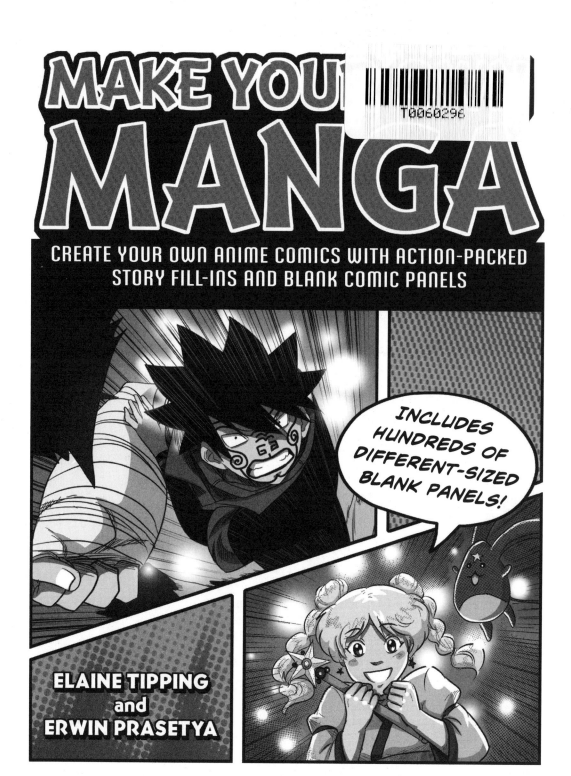

MAKE YOUR MANGA

CREATE YOUR OWN ANIME COMICS WITH ACTION-PACKED
STORY FILL-INS AND BLANK COMIC PANELS

INCLUDES HUNDREDS OF DIFFERENT-SIZED BLANK PANELS!

ELAINE TIPPING
and
ERWIN PRASETYA

Adams Media
New York   London   Toronto   Sydney   New Delhi

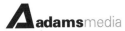

Adams Media
An Imprint of Simon & Schuster, Inc.
100 Technology Center Drive
Stoughton, Massachusetts 02072

First Adams Media trade paperback edition June 2021

ADAMS MEDIA and colophon are trademarks of Simon & Schuster.

For information about special discounts for bulk purchases, please contact Simon & Schuster Special Sales at 1-866-506-1949 or business@simonandschuster.com.

The Simon & Schuster Speakers Bureau can bring authors to your live event. For more information or to book an event contact the Simon & Schuster Speakers Bureau at 1-866-248-3049 or visit our website at www.simonspeakers.com.

Interior design by Colleen Cunningham
Interior illustrations by Elaine Tipping and Erwin Prasetya
Interior images © Getty Images/helen_tosh; 123RF/alexslb, dgool, Dmitry Larichev, valeriyador

Manufactured in the United States of America

2 2022

ISBN 978-1-5072-1651-4

Contains material adapted from the following title published by Adams Media, an Imprint of Simon & Schuster, Inc.: *Make Your Own Manga* by Elaine Tipping, Gar Molloy, Robin Edwards, and Erwin Prasetya, copyright © 2013, ISBN 978-1-4405-5782-8.

CONTENTS

INTRODUCTION

You've never seen manga like this before!

Are your bookshelves crammed with every issue of *Demon Slayer*? Were you amazed by the latest production from Studio Ghibli? No matter which story is your favorite, you know that manga and anime entertain you the way nothing else can.

But after tearing through your favorite series, what's next? You want to start making your own manga *right now*!

That's where *Make Your Own Manga* comes in. This isn't a book of manga to read. It's a book of manga to create and write! We provide the format; you provide the drawings and story.

Flip through this book, and you'll see that we've got it all. *Shoujo*-style girls with big *kawaii* eyes, and *shounen*-style ninjas with a taste for justice. Whether you're a fan of *Naruto* or *Fruits Basket*, *Fullmetal Alchemist* or *One Piece*, you'll find your favorite styles and stories. Adventure, romance, fantasy, and science fiction—it's all here.

As you'll see in Part I, there's one big difference between this manga and your favorite series: The word bubbles in the drawings are blank.

All the manga has been drawn by well-known manga and anime artists Elaine Tipping and Erwin Prasetya. Glance through the illustrations and let your imagination run wild. What's the spunky schoolgirl's secret? Who's the boy riding on a kite and playing with the clouds? Why does the nerdy girl have a crush on the handsome boy? You'll find friendly animal sidekicks, daring samurai, high school crushes, and so much more. And for the first time, you control the story. Is the star of your manga a ruthless antihero or an earnest do-gooder? Is that schoolgirl thinking about her boyfriend or the code to top-secret government files? That's up to you to decide!

Take a look at the second part of the book: This is not just about writing manga; it's also about drawing it. In fact, you may even want to start with this part of the book. In Part II, you can let your imagination run wild as you push the boundaries of what's possible. Draw your own illustrations for your own stories. We've provided a template for you; now it's up to you to create exciting content, both drawings and stories!

There's no limit—you get to decide.

HOW TO USE THIS BOOK

At this point, you may be wondering: What do I need to make my own manga? It's very simple. Here's all you need:

1. This book.
2. A pencil.
3. Your brain.

It's easy. Let's say you decide you want to do Part I first. Flip through the stories—the ones with illustrations—and decide what you want to write. Then grab a pen or pencil and start the fill-in fun.

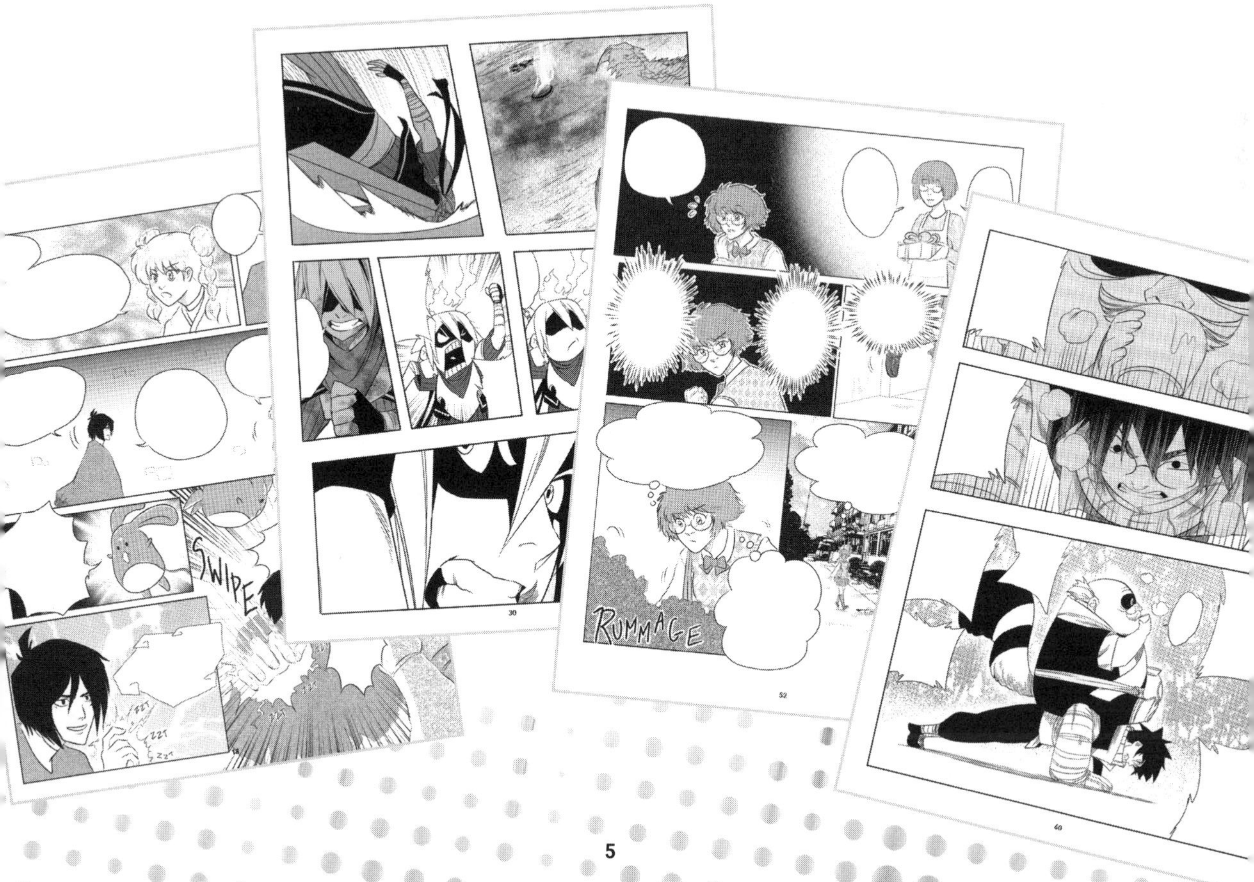
SWIPE
RUMMAGE

Here are a few panels from story #4 in Part I:

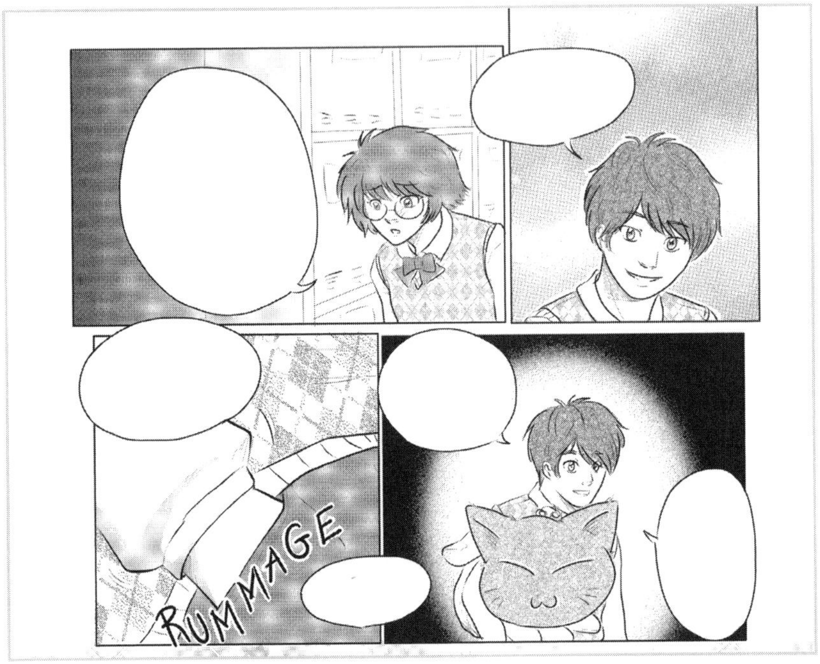
RUMMAGE

And here's what it might look like when you're done with it:

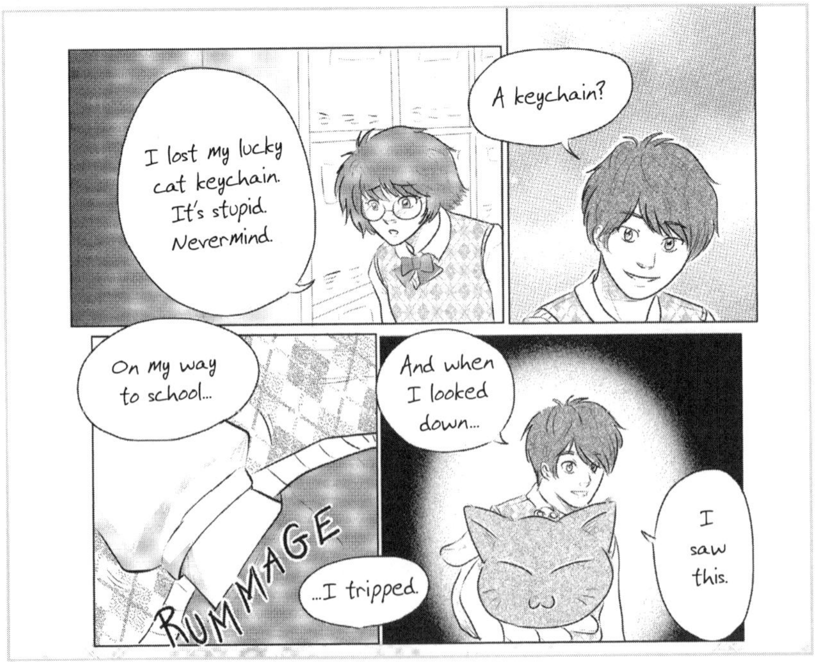
I lost my lucky cat keychain. It's stupid. Nevermind.
A keychain?
On my way to school...
RUMMAGE
...I tripped.
And when I looked down...
I saw this.

Or, if you're in a different kind of mood, it might look more like this:

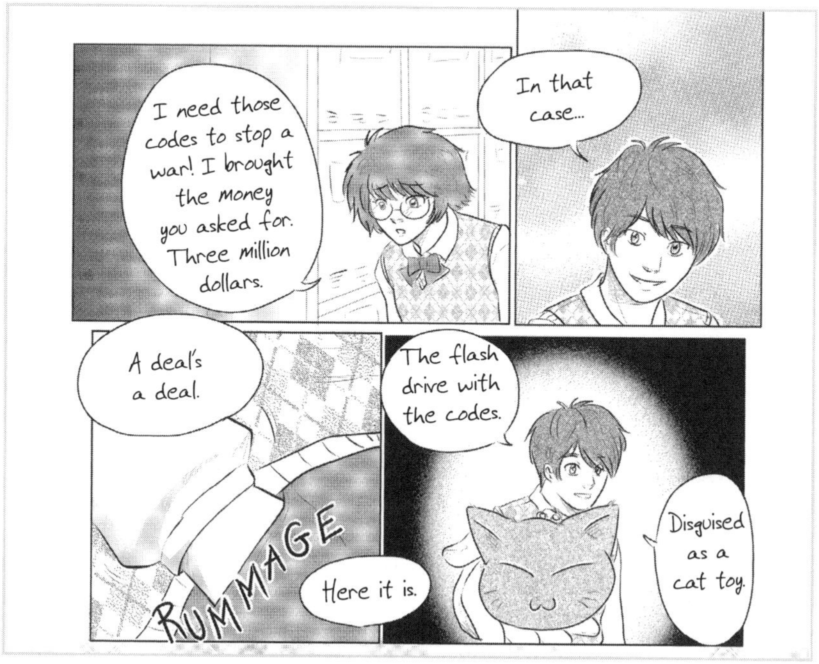
I need those codes to stop a war! I brought the money you asked for. Three million dollars.
In that case...
A deal's a deal.
RUMMAGE
Here it is.
The flash drive with the codes.
Disguised as a cat toy.

The more manga stories you write, the better they'll be and the easier you'll find the process. Go back to the stories you wrote earlier and see how the drawings can be interpreted in different ways. Which of these alternate stories do you like best? There's no right answer—just look for the one that really sparks your imagination!

What if you decide you'd rather work on Part II of the book first? Here you'll find a series of blank panels, just waiting for you to go to work on them. In this part, you can write your own story (or stories) *and* you can *draw* your own panels to illustrate your narratives.

Maybe you'll get some ideas from your favorite manga artists. Or you can simply tap in to your own creativity to show what the characters in your head are doing. Don't worry about producing top-level drawings. The goal is just to have fun.

Above all, rely on your imagination. Thinking of a battle beyond the stars? Sketch it out. Do your characters find hidden aspects of themselves at school or in the park? Draw that and write down the story. Are your heroes and heroines brave knights of long ago? Show them battling for power. There's a big panel (or a couple of big panels) to start things off with a bang, and end with a flourish.

Here’s a sample of a couple of story pages in Part II:

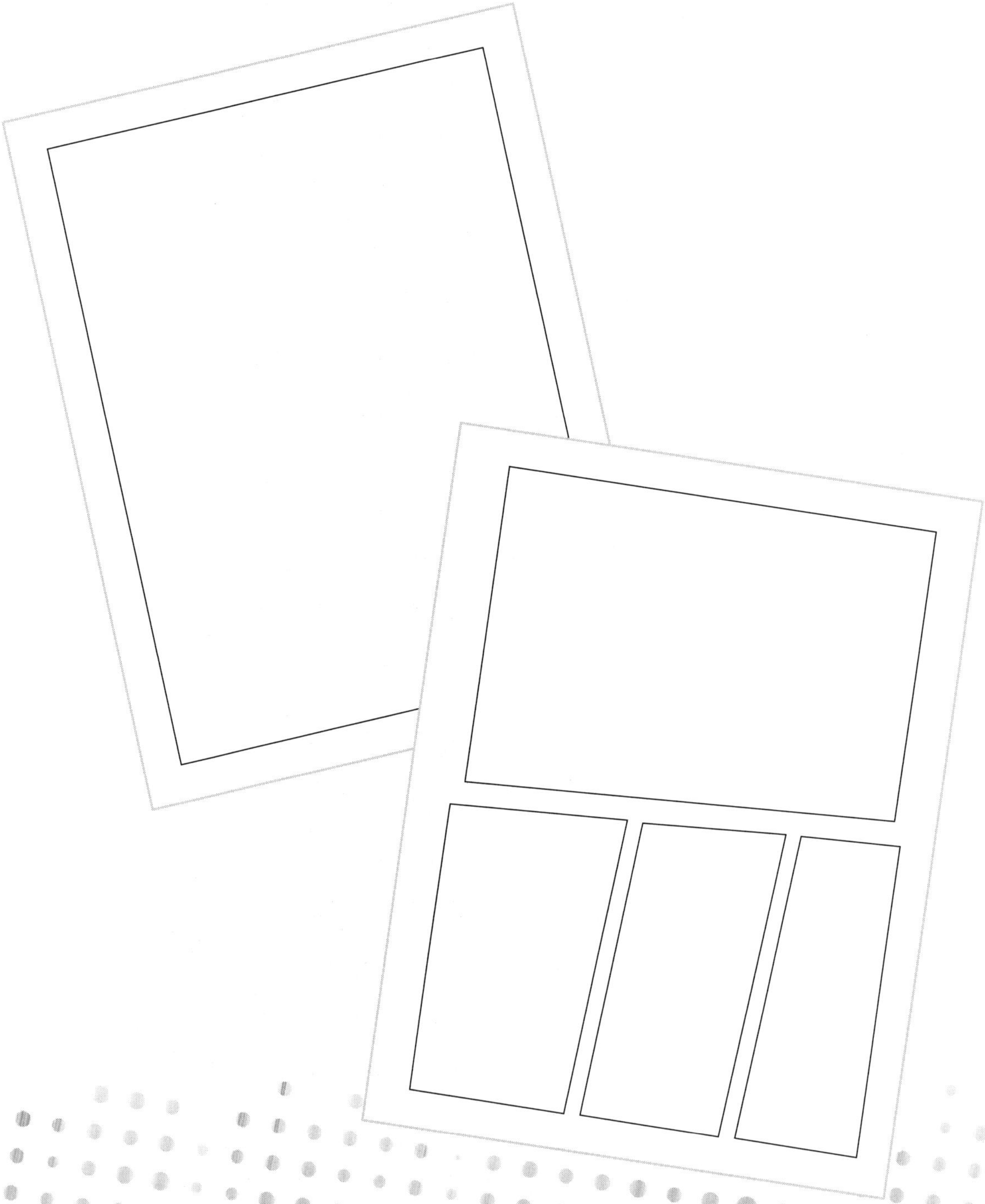

And here's what those pages might look like when you're done with them:

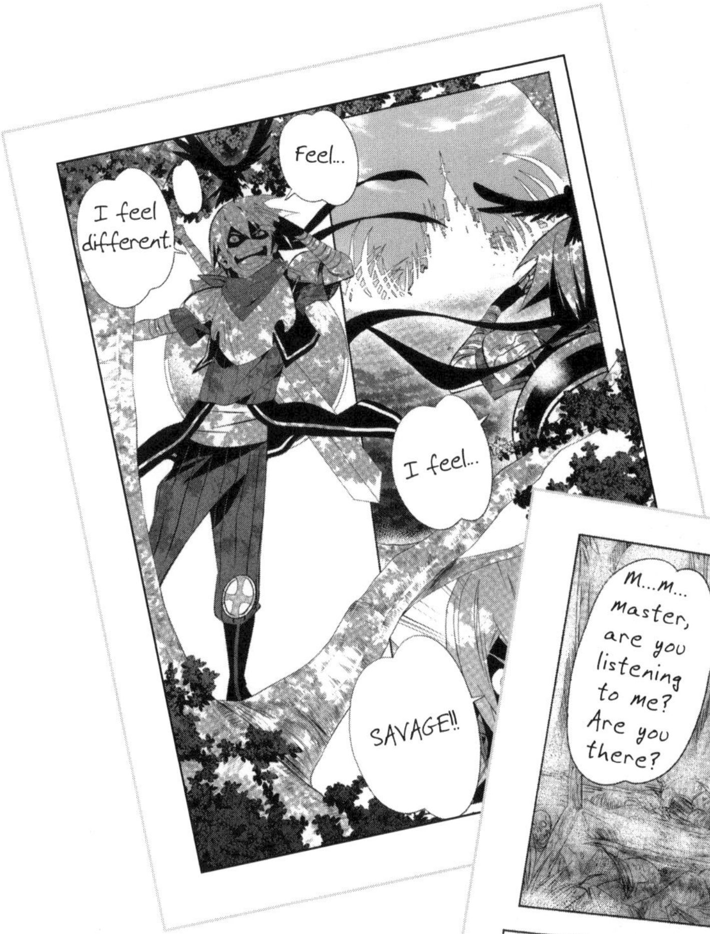
Feel...
I feel different.
I feel...
SAVAGE!!

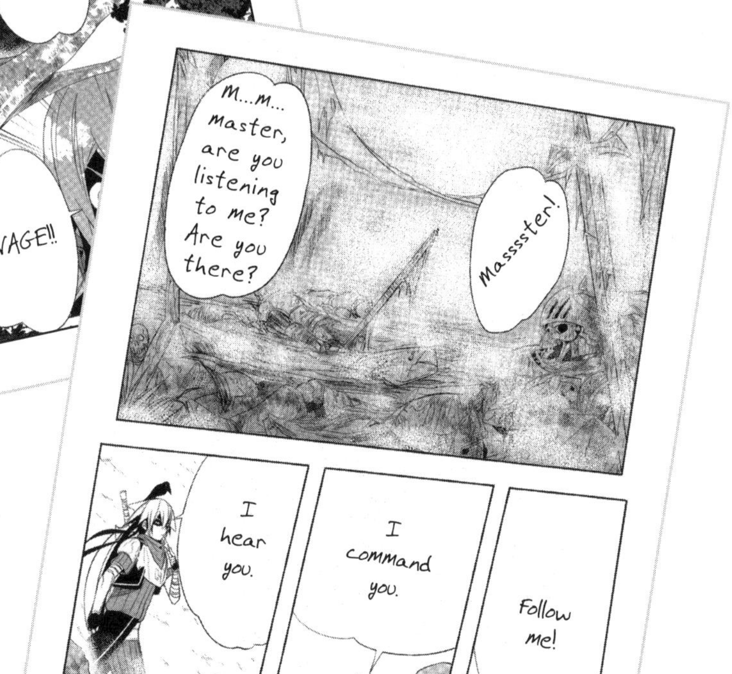
M...M... master, are you listening to me? Are you there?
Masssster!
I hear you.
I command you.
Follow me!

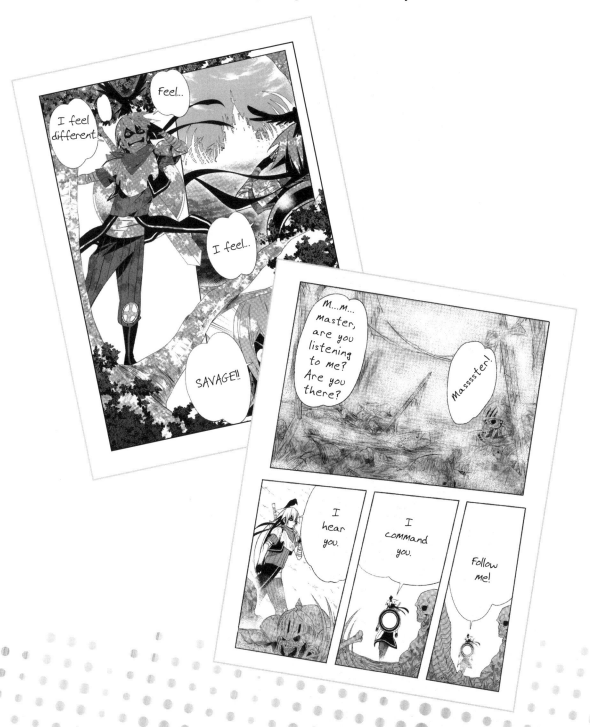

Whether you're a serious *otaku* or just getting started, whether you want to tell serious stories or just have a blast writing the silliest thing you can think of, *Make Your Own Manga* is the book for you. So turn the page and start creating!

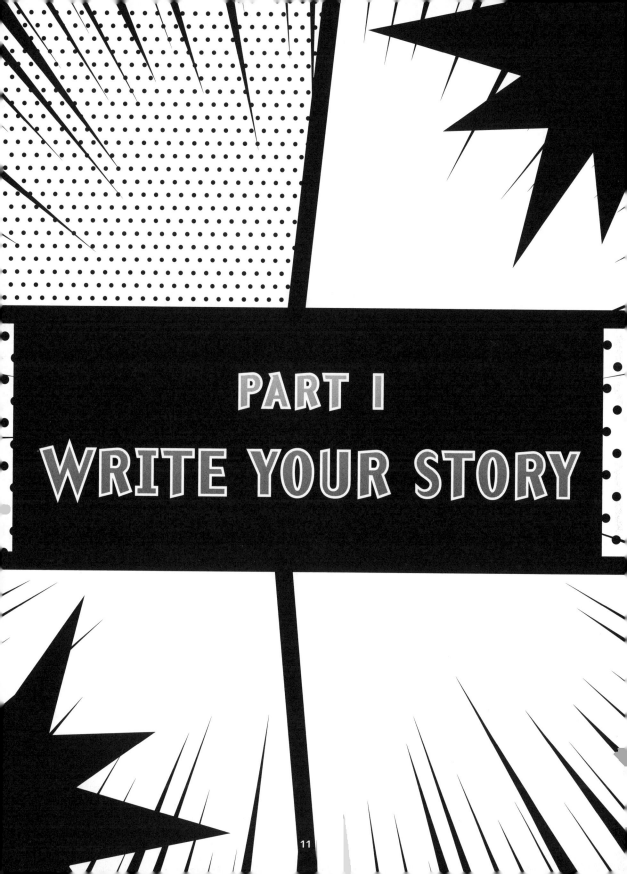

PART I
WRITE YOUR STORY

If you feel like it, start with this part of *Make Your Own Manga*. You can use the drawings of manga artists as inspiration for your stories. Look at the people or creatures in the panels, think about what they might be doing or saying, and then write in the words. Does your story have a beginning and an ending? Is there a villain, or do two people (or a person and a creature) link up to defeat evil?

STORY #1

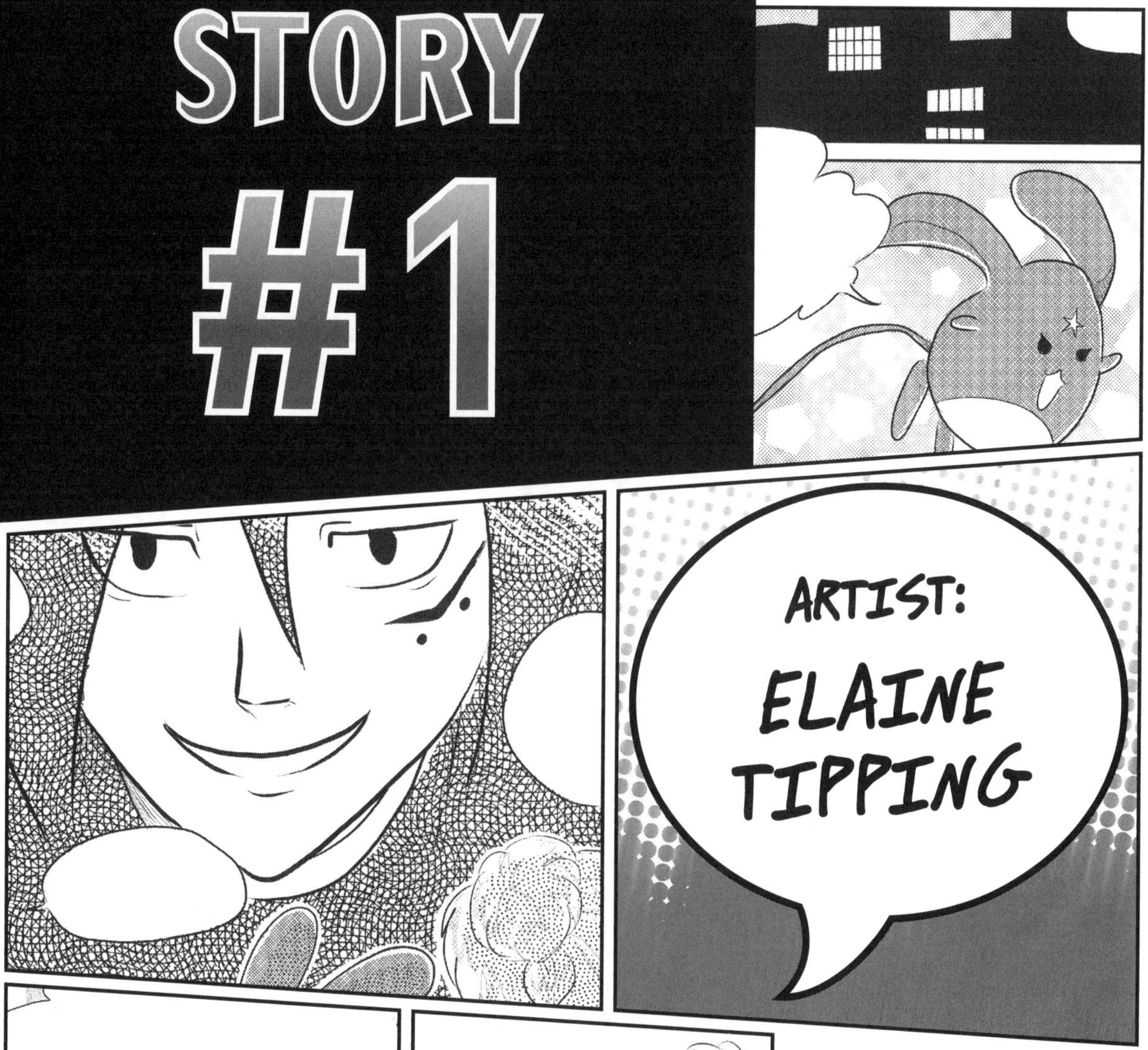
ARTIST:
ELAINE TIPPING

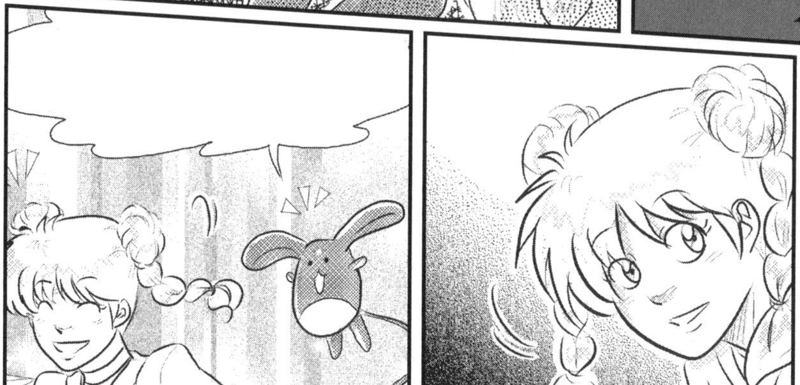

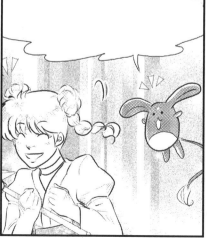

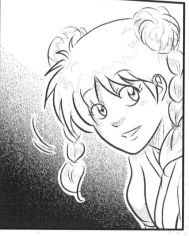

TITLE:

____

____

____

WRITER:

____

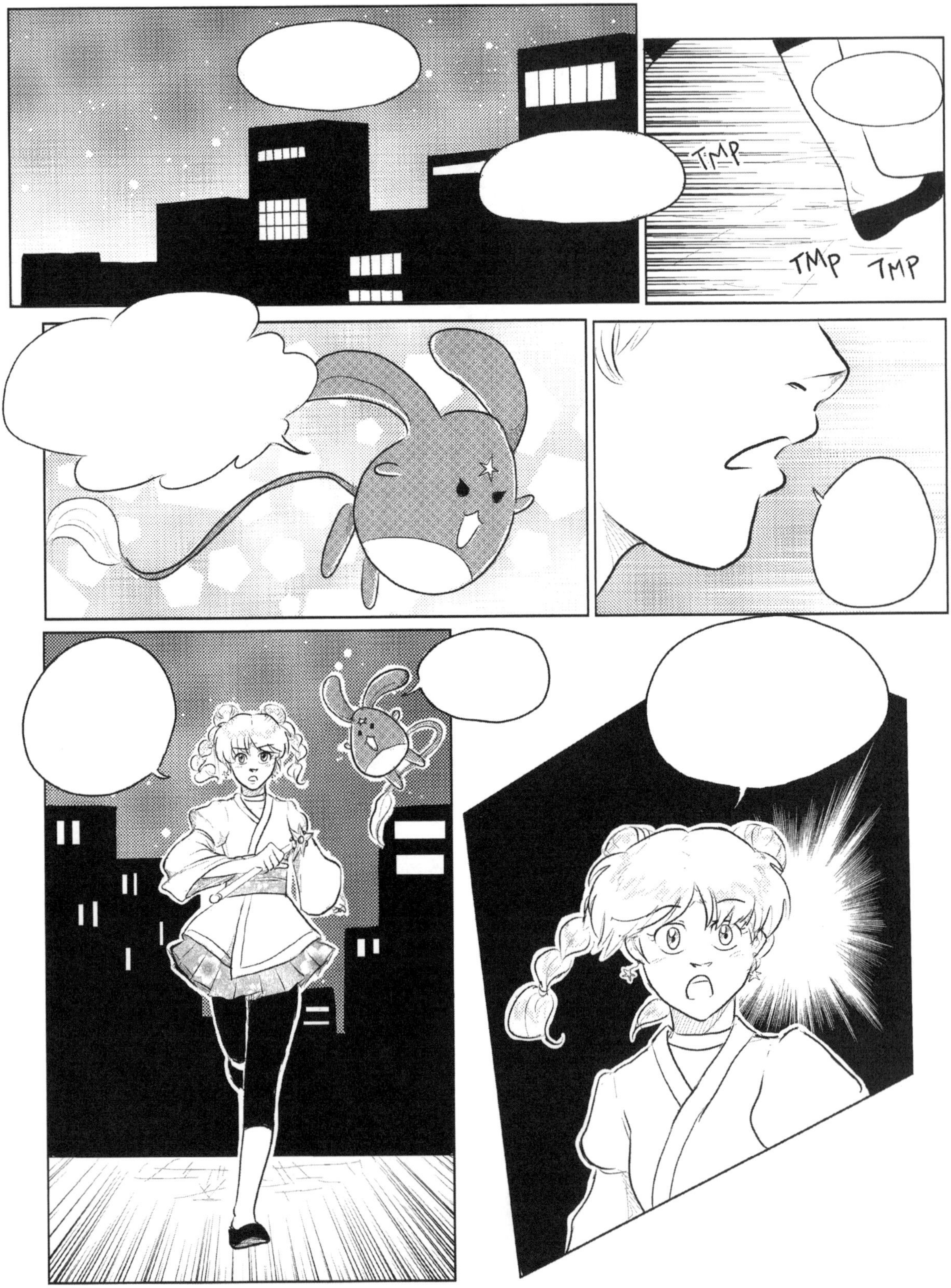
TMP
TMP
TMP

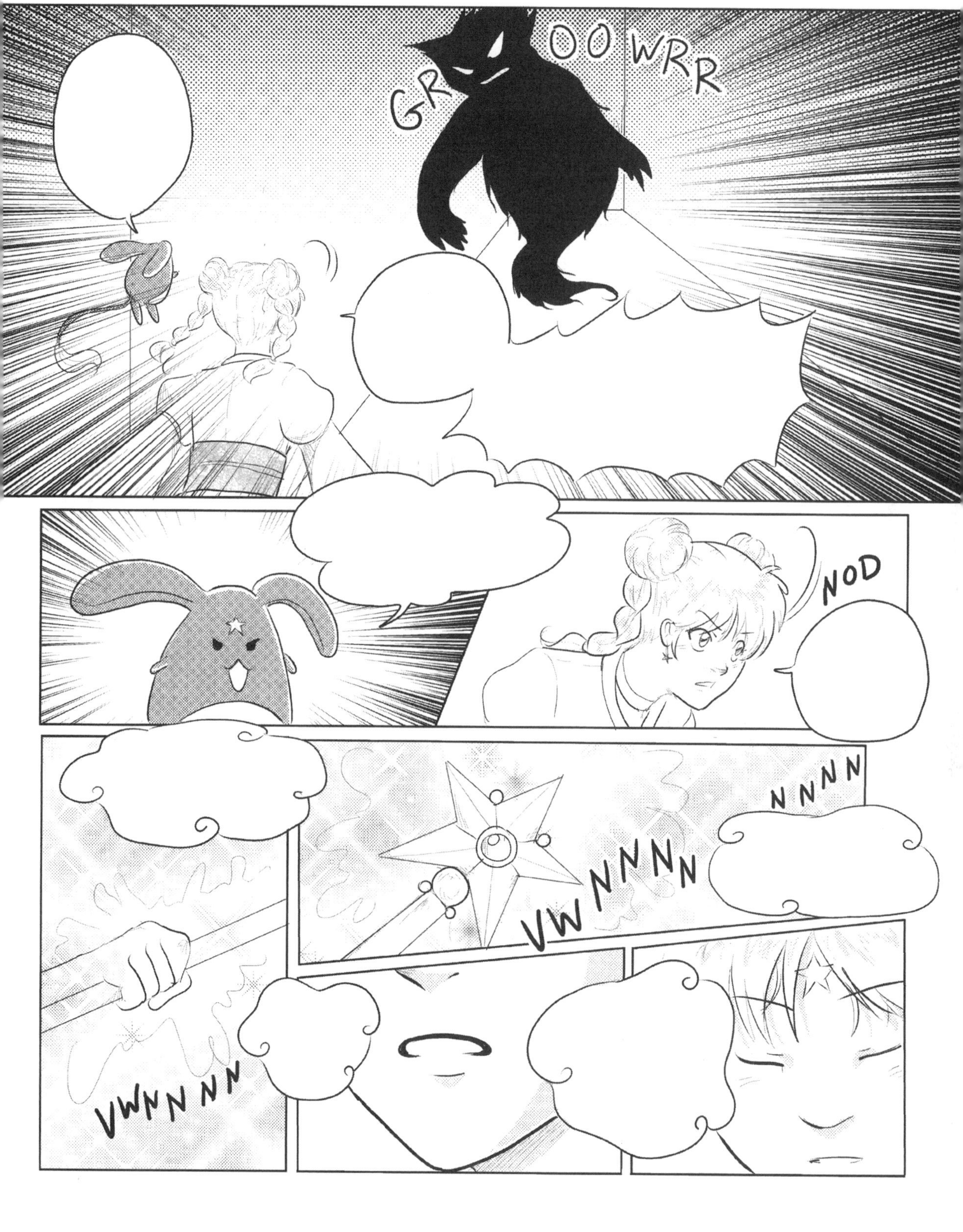
GR OO WRR
NOD
NNNN
VWNNNNN
VWNNNN

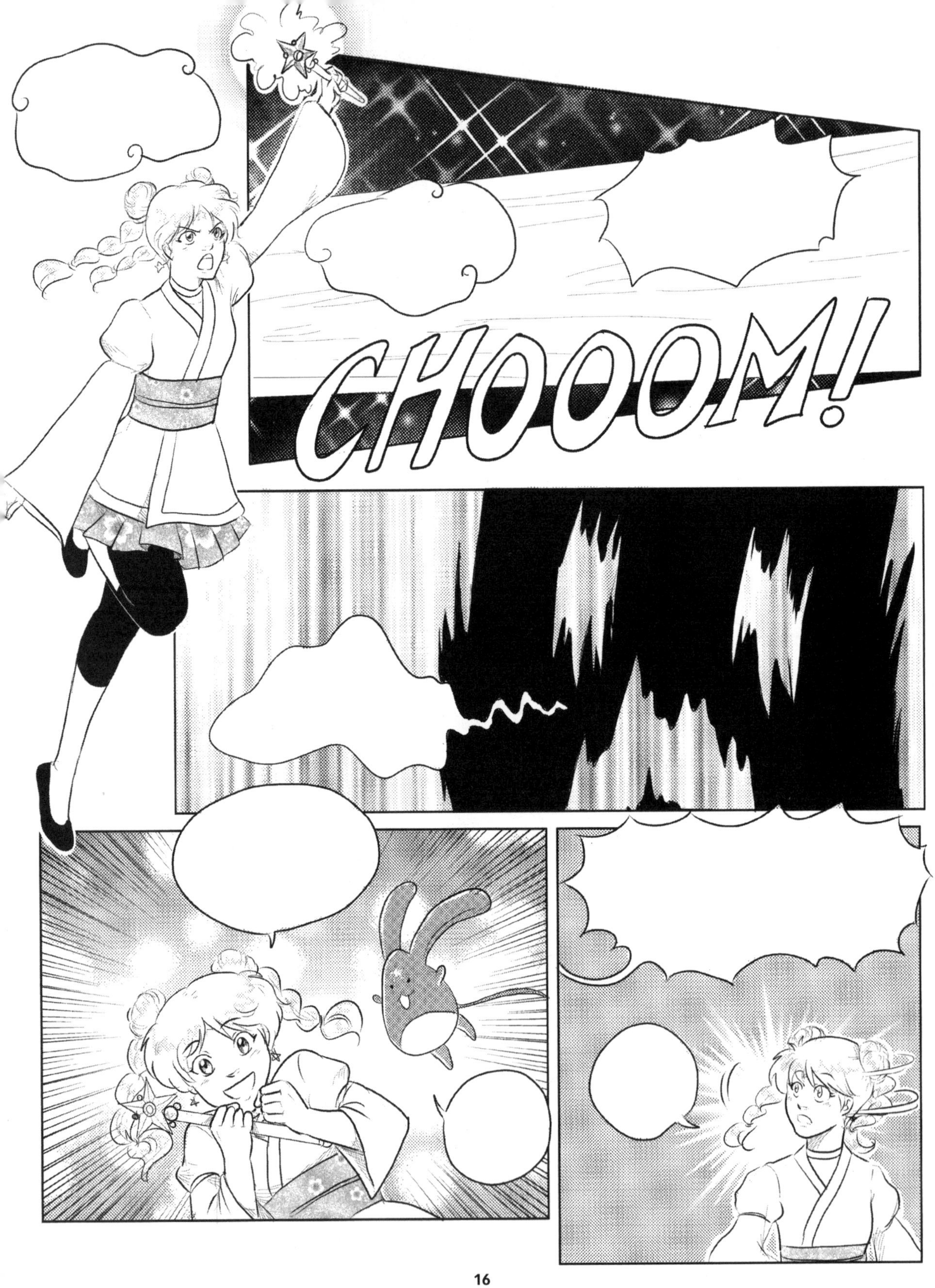
CHOOOM!

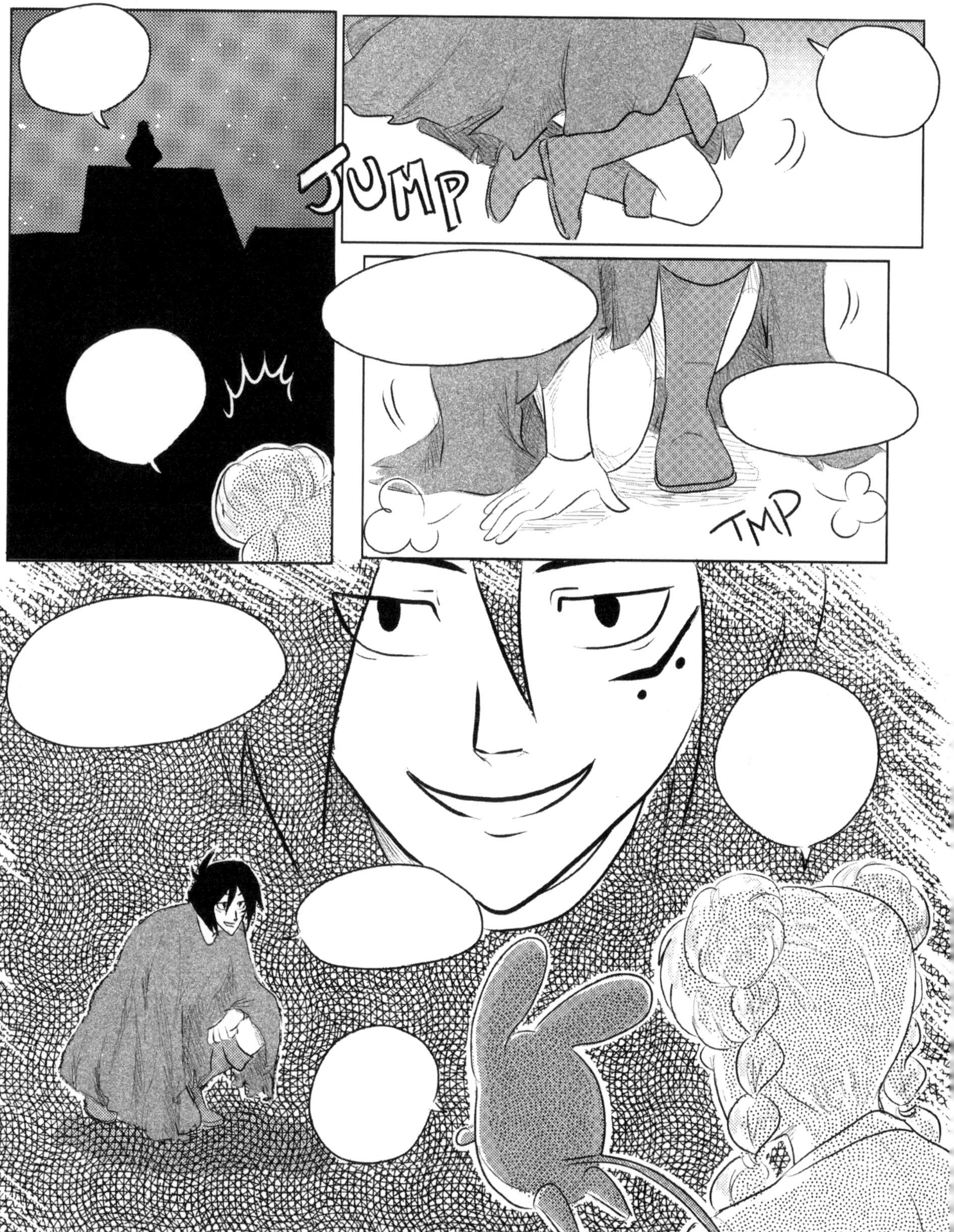
JUMP
TMP

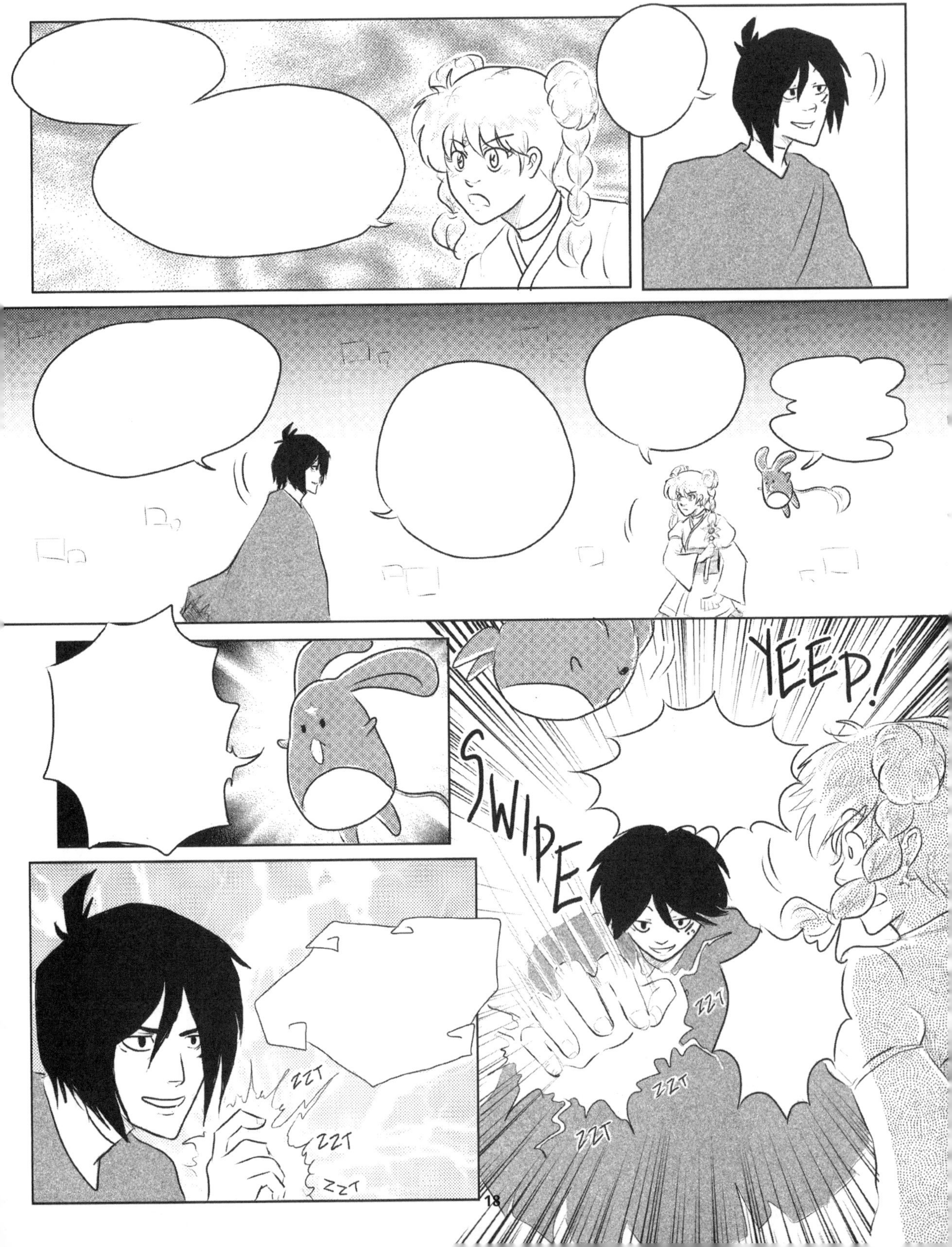
YEEP!
SWIPE
ZZT
ZZT
ZZT
ZZT
ZZT
ZZT

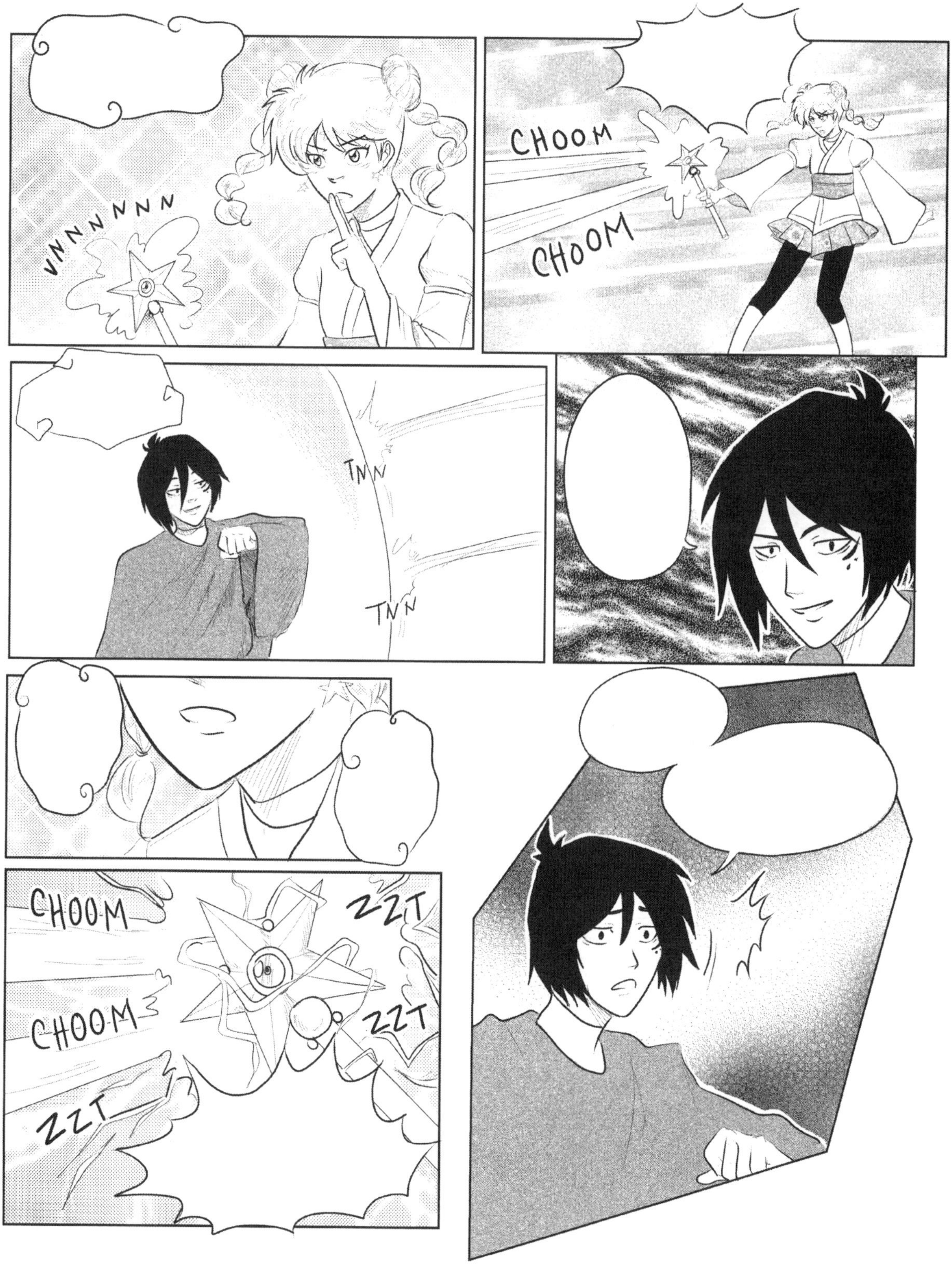
VNNNNNNN
CHOOM
CHOOM
TNN
TNN
CHOOM
ZZT
CHOOM
ZZT
ZZT

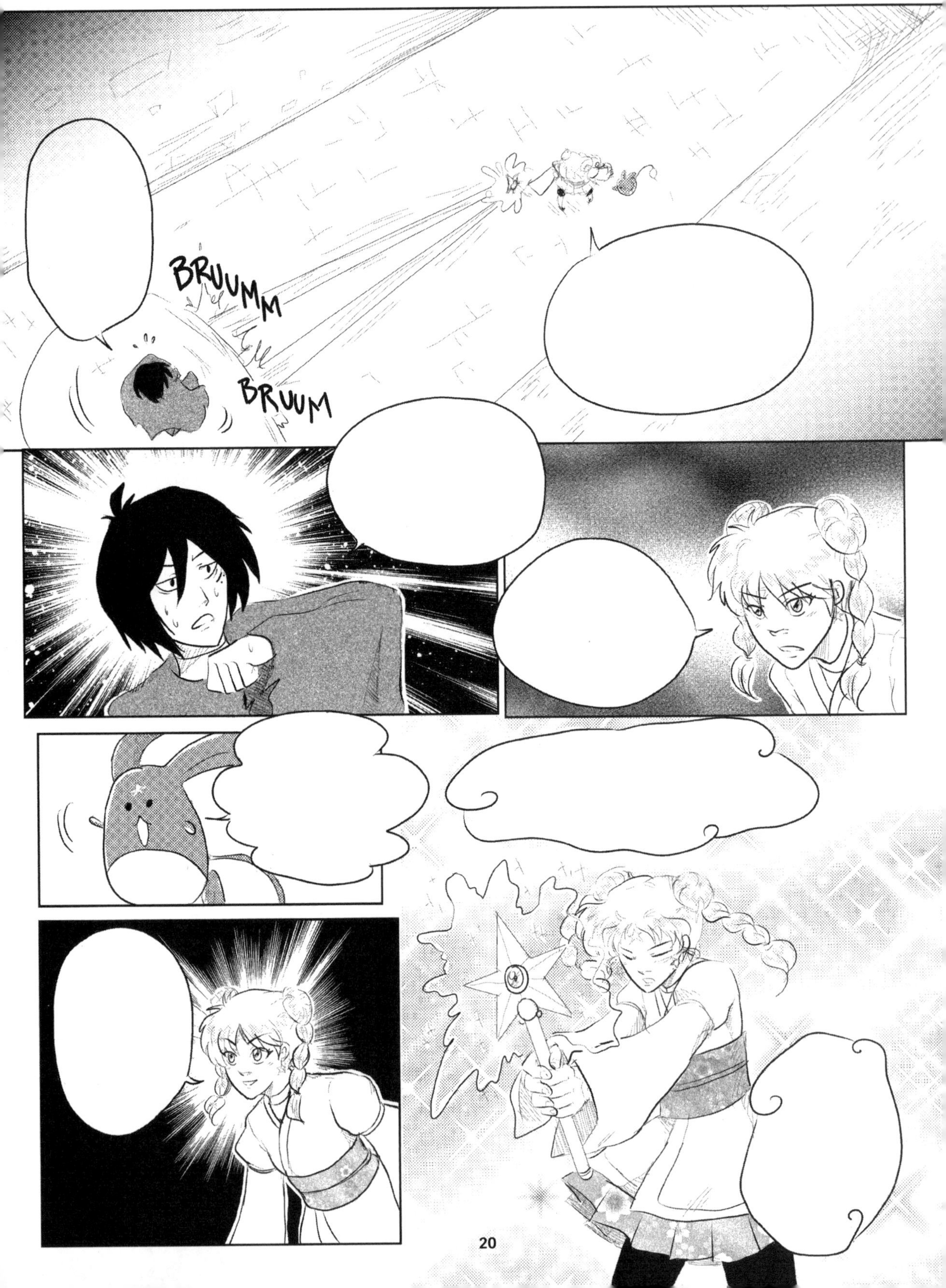
BRUUMM
BRUUM

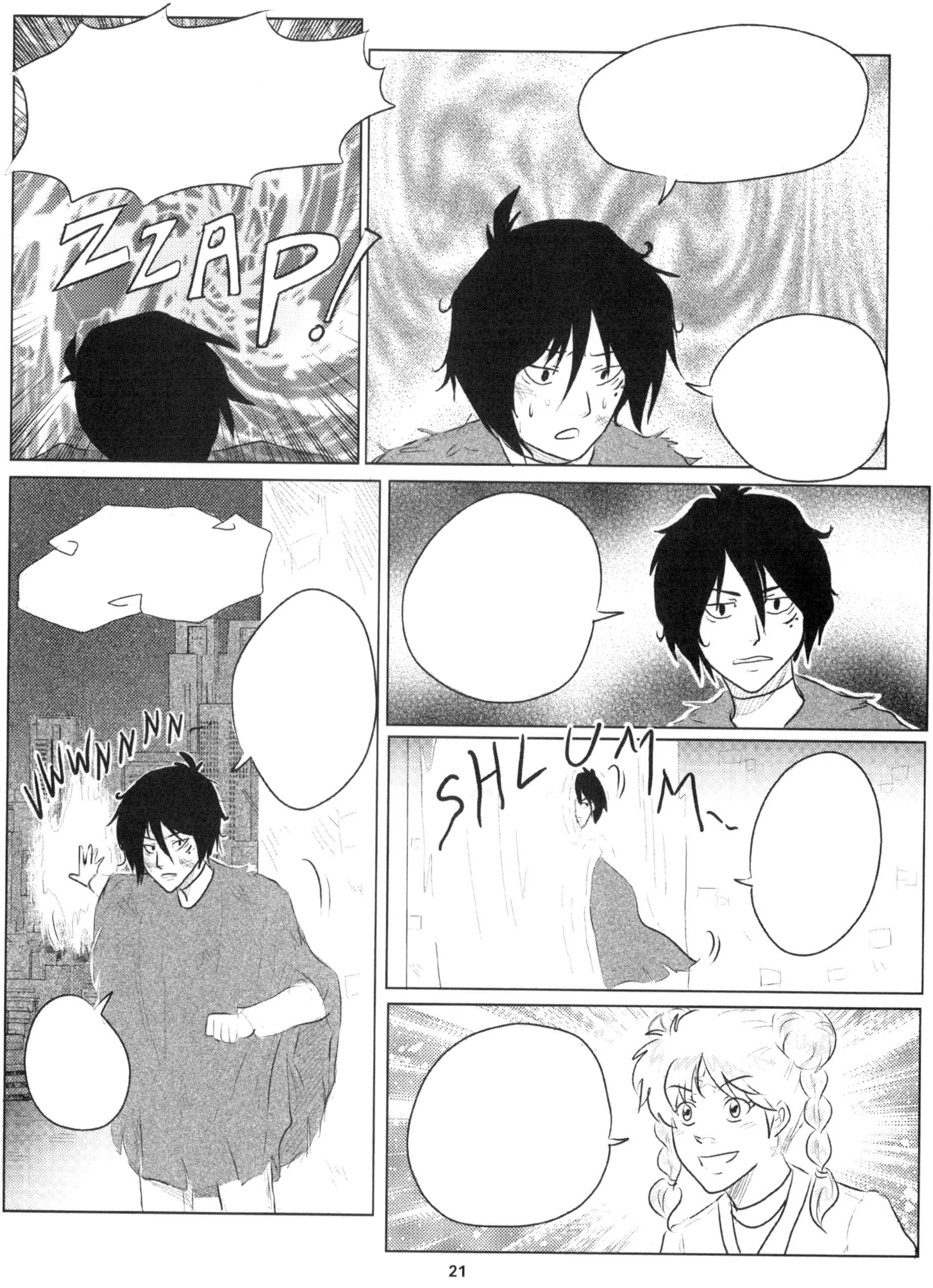
ZZAP!
VWWNNNN~
SHLUMM~

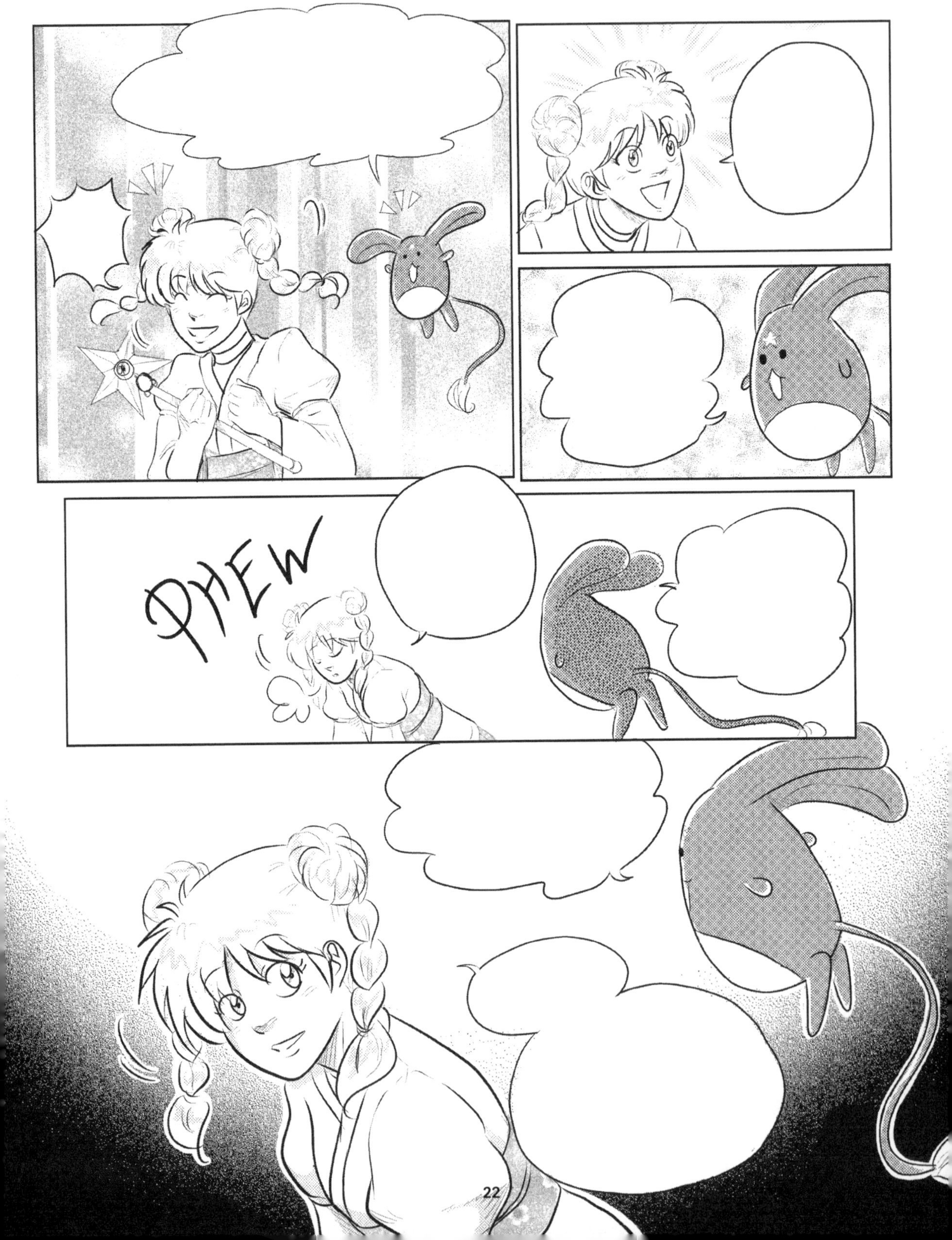
PHEW

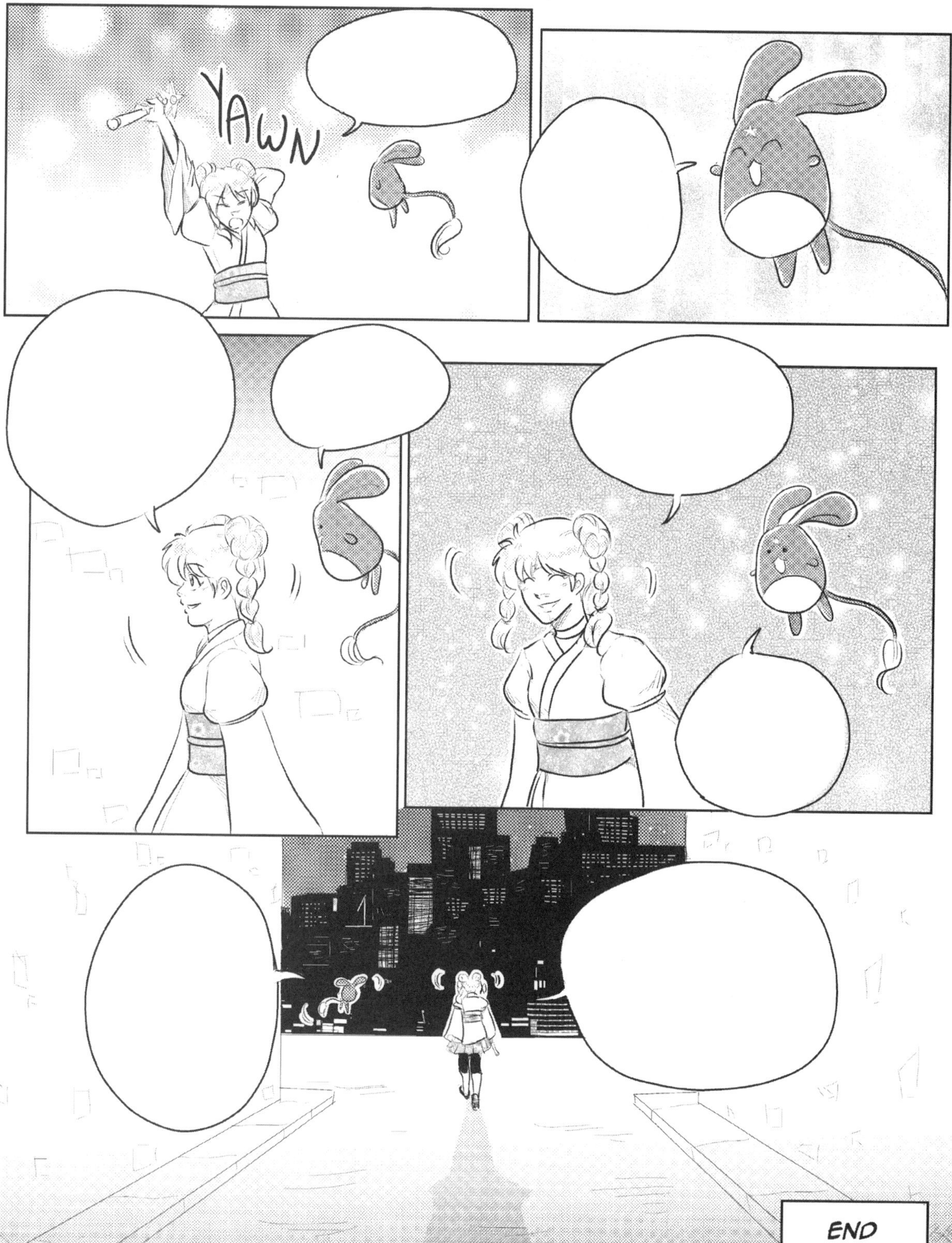
YAWN
END

STORY #2

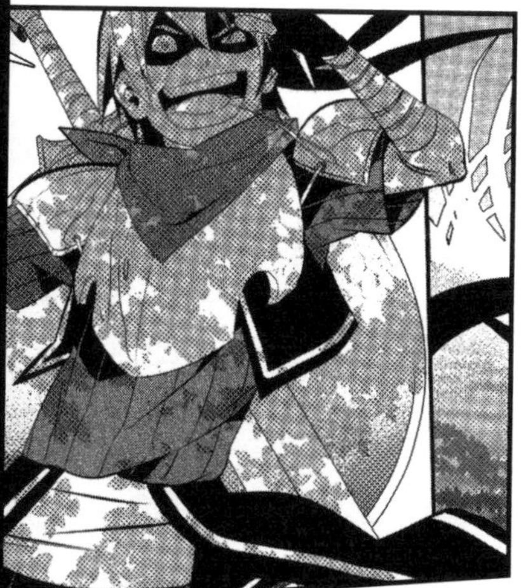

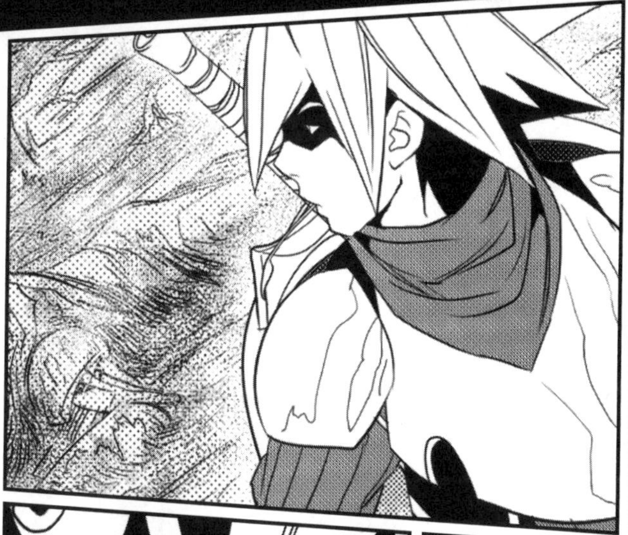

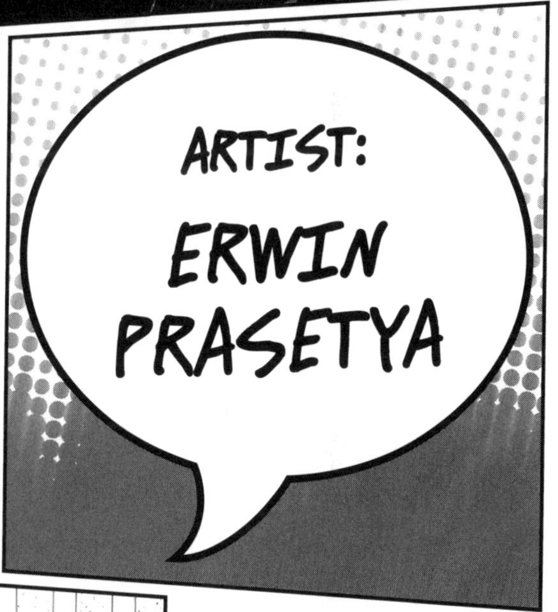
ARTIST:
ERWIN PRASETYA

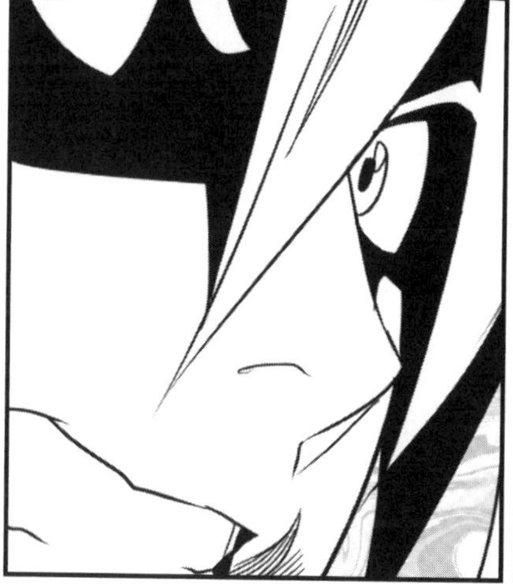

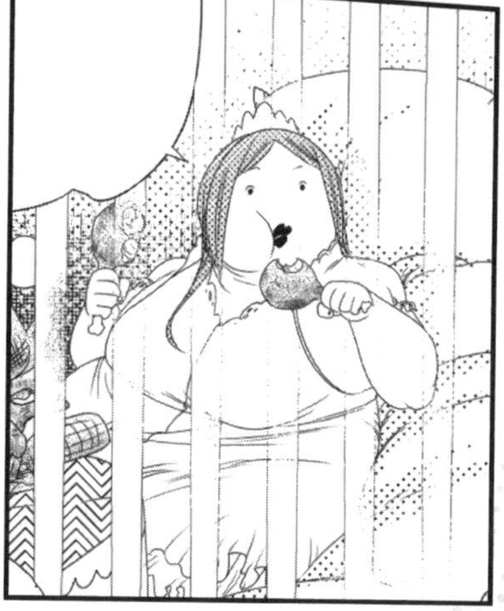

TITLE:

WRITER:

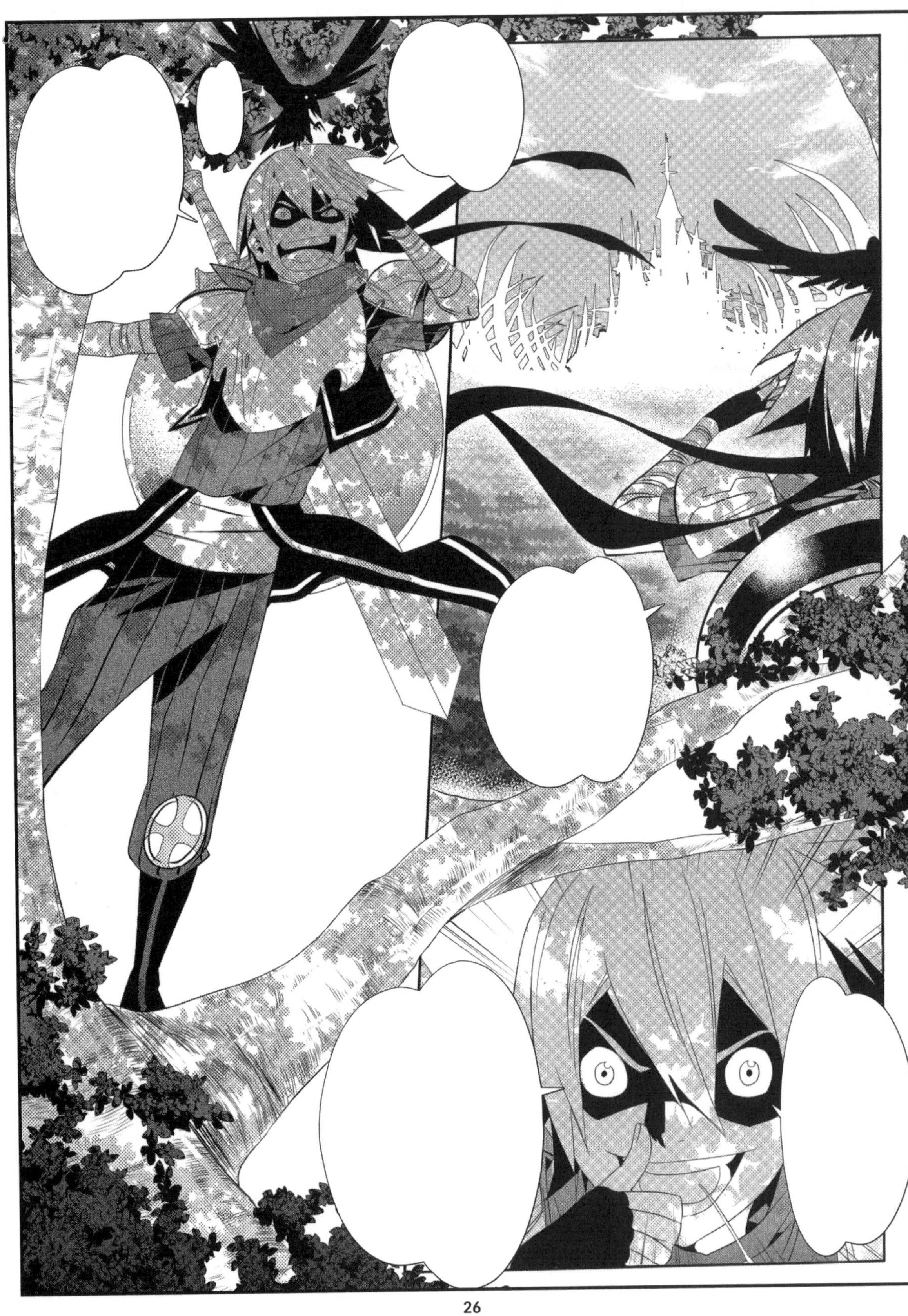

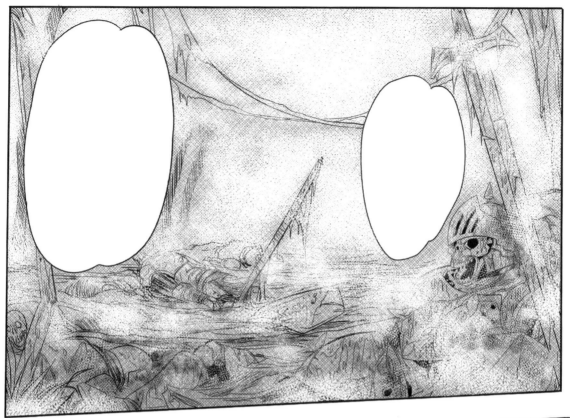

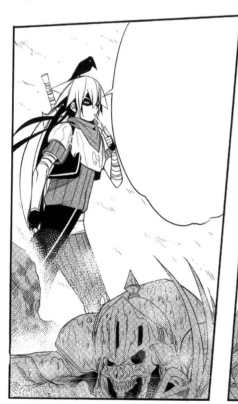

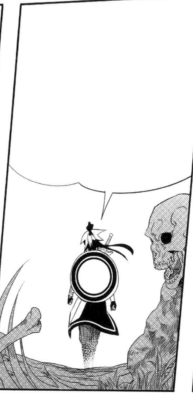

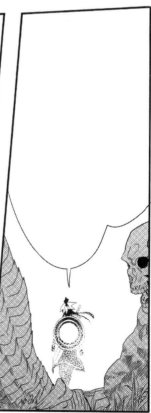

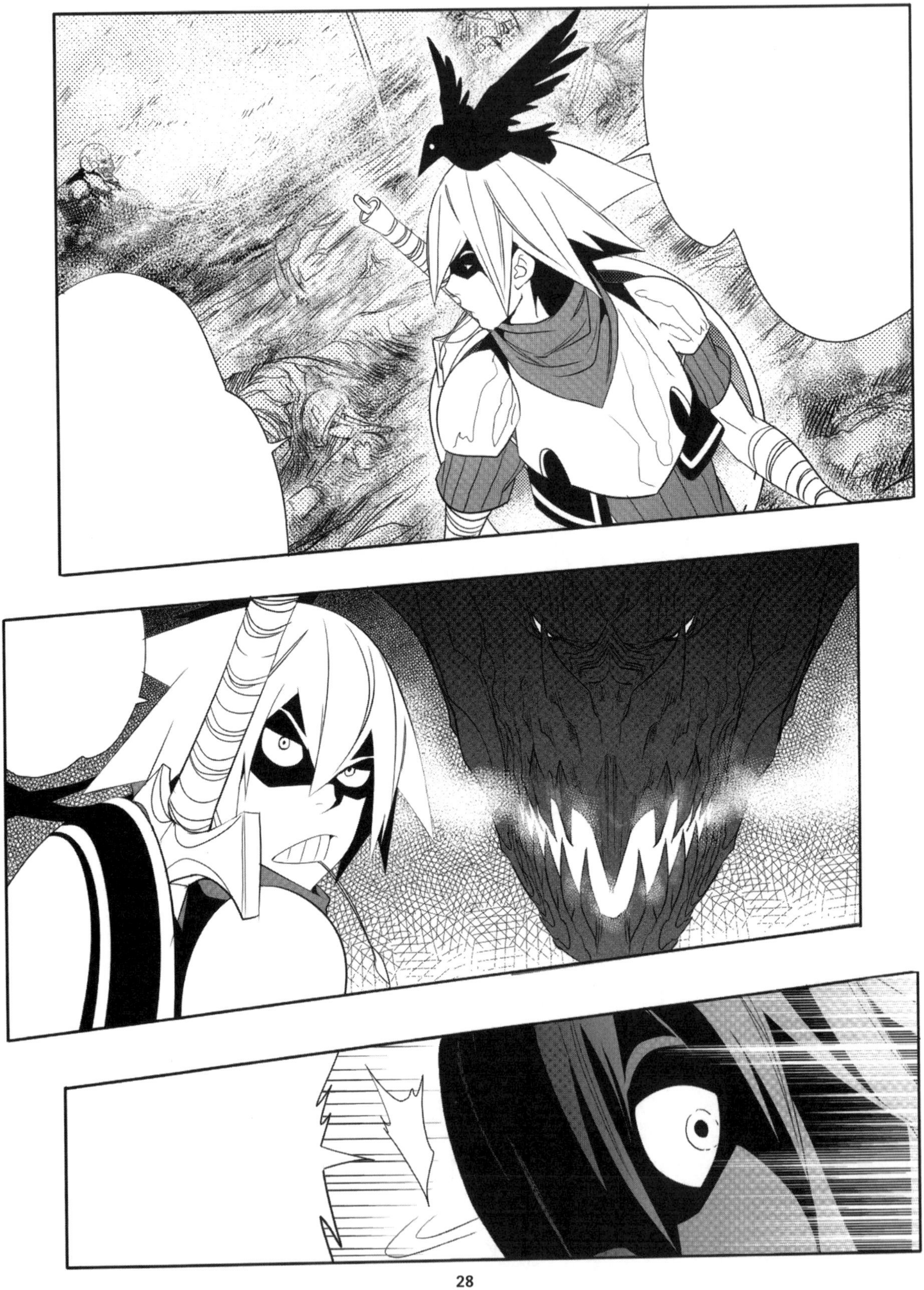

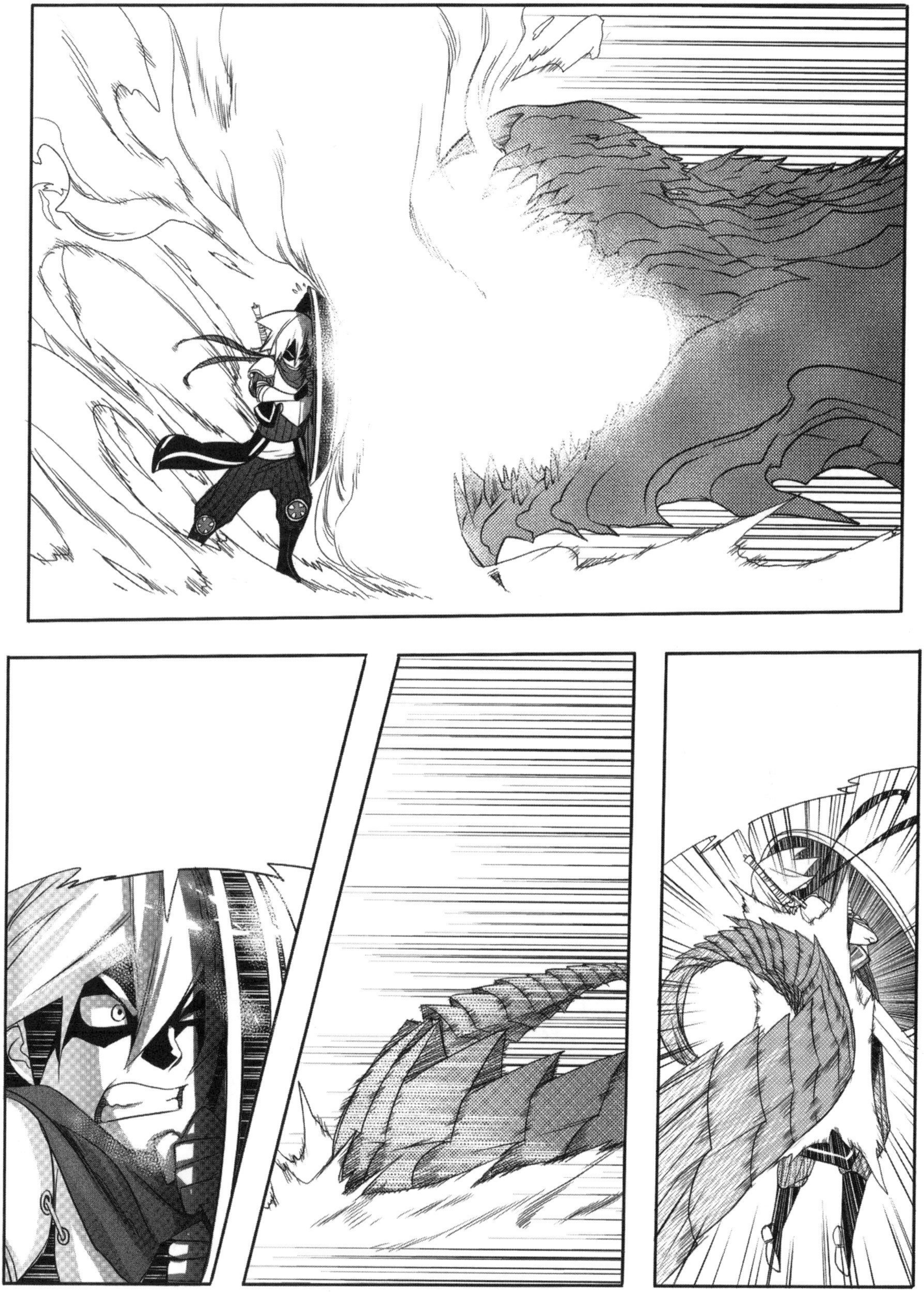

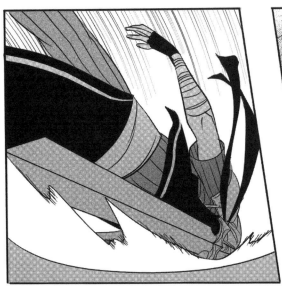
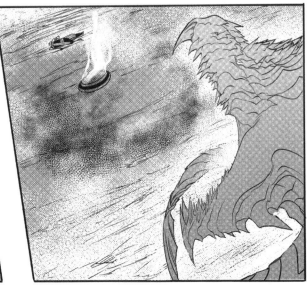
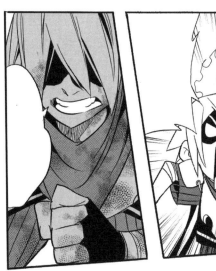
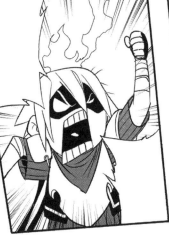
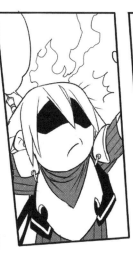
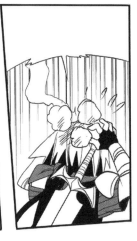
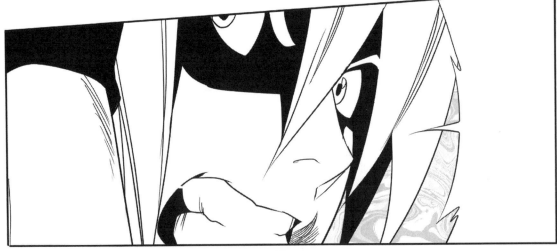

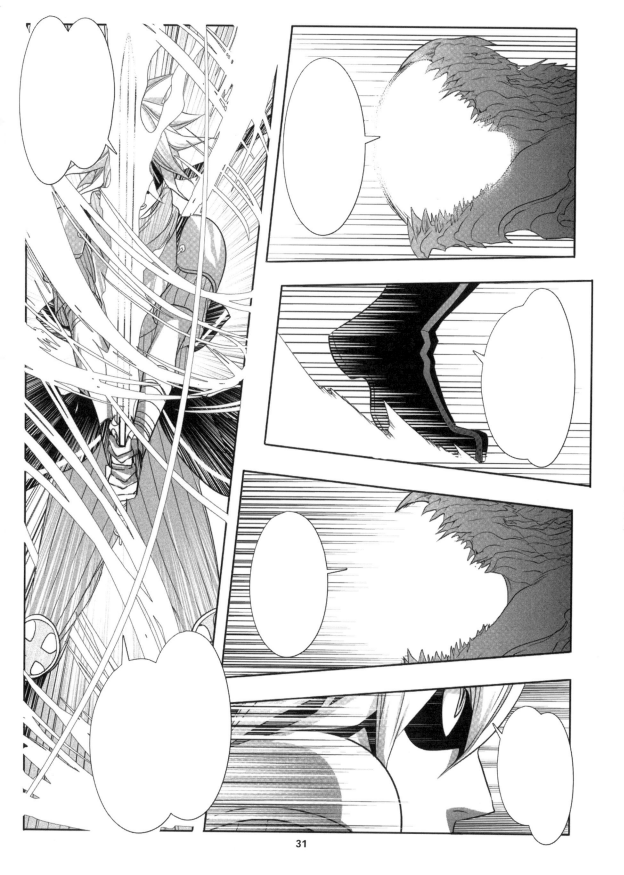

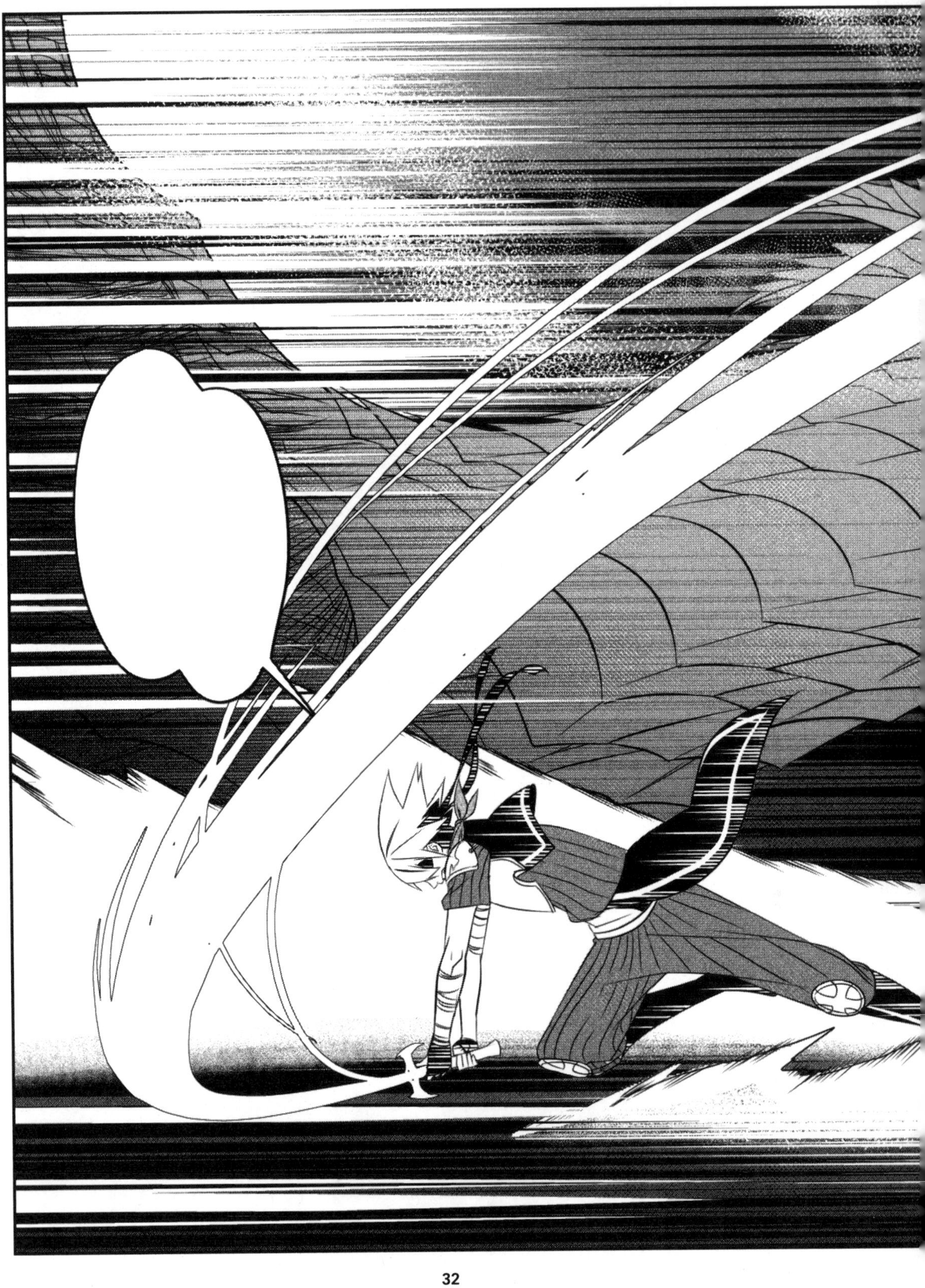

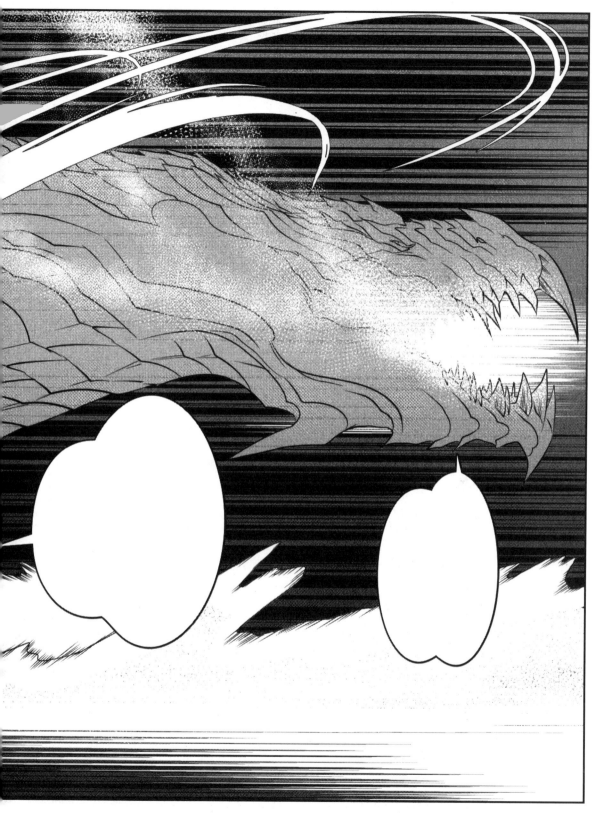

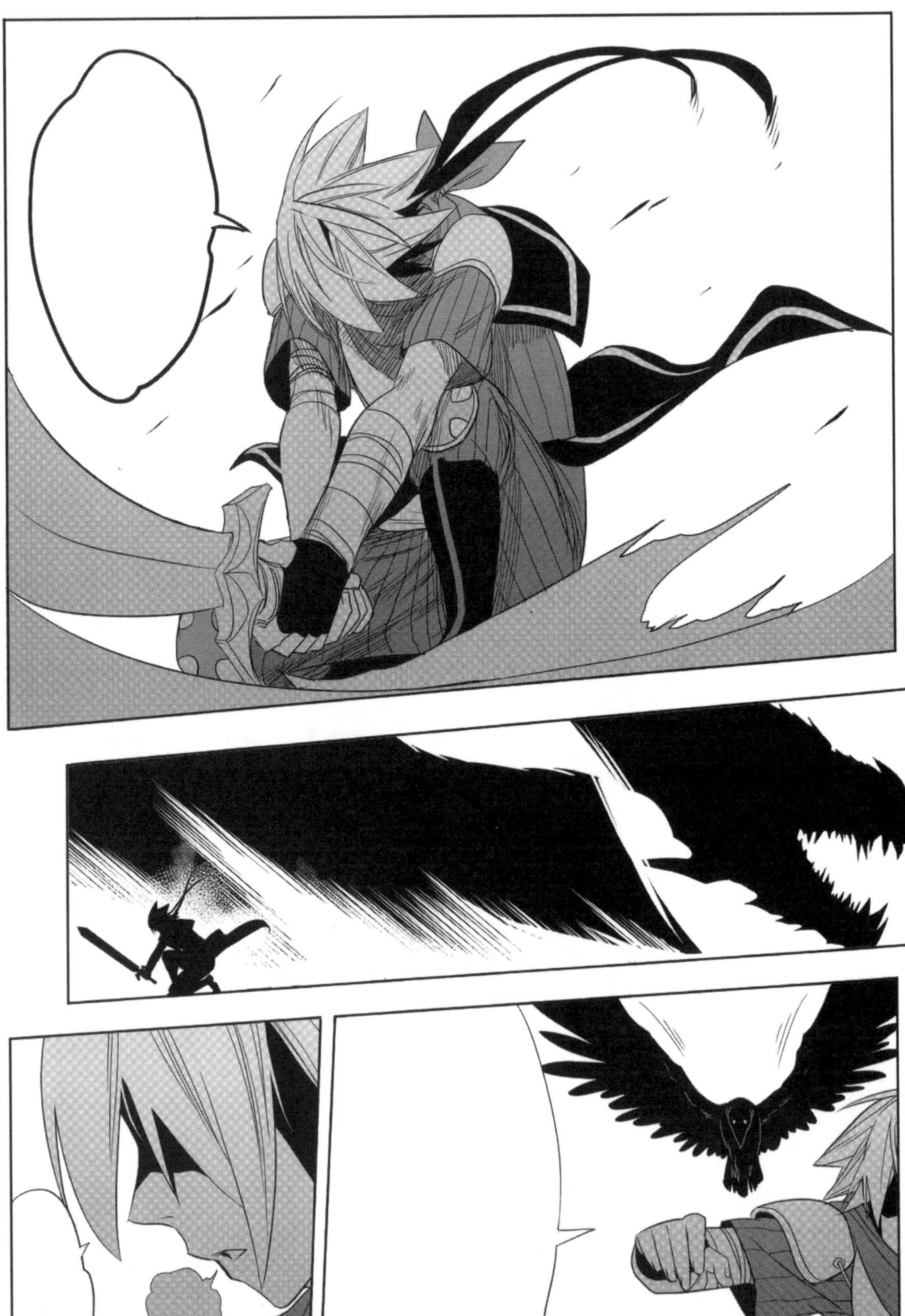

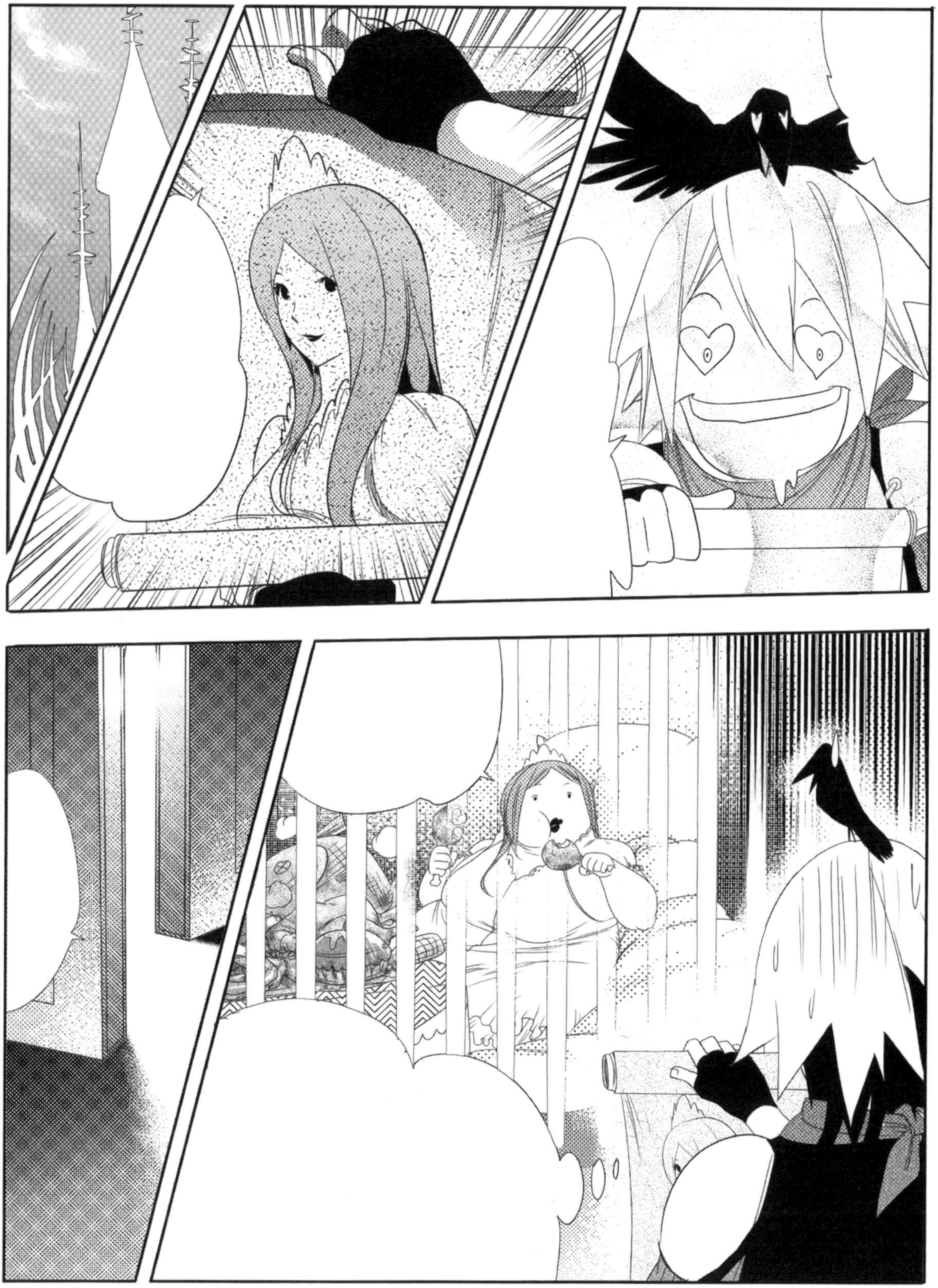

STORY #3

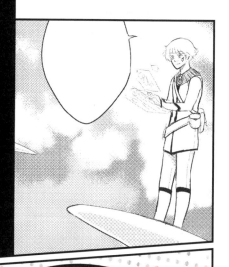

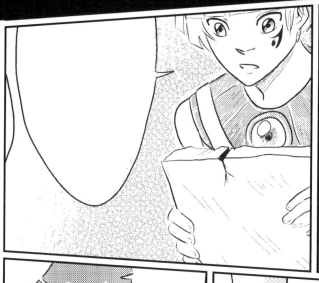

ARTIST:

ELAINE TIPPING

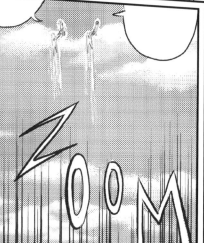

ZOOM

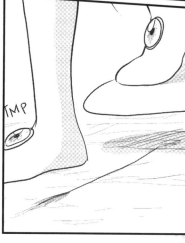

TMP

TITLE:

_____

_____

WRITER:

_____

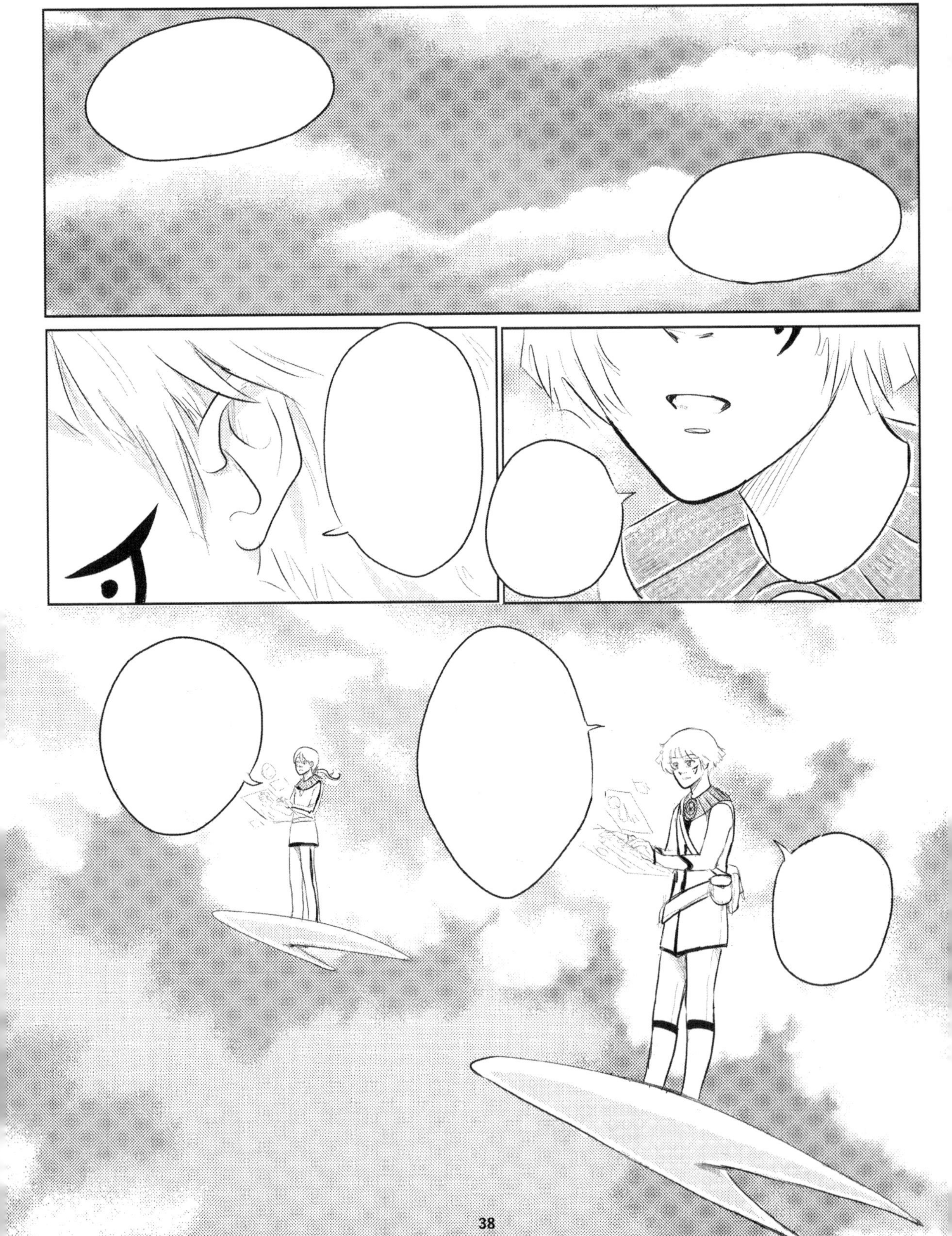

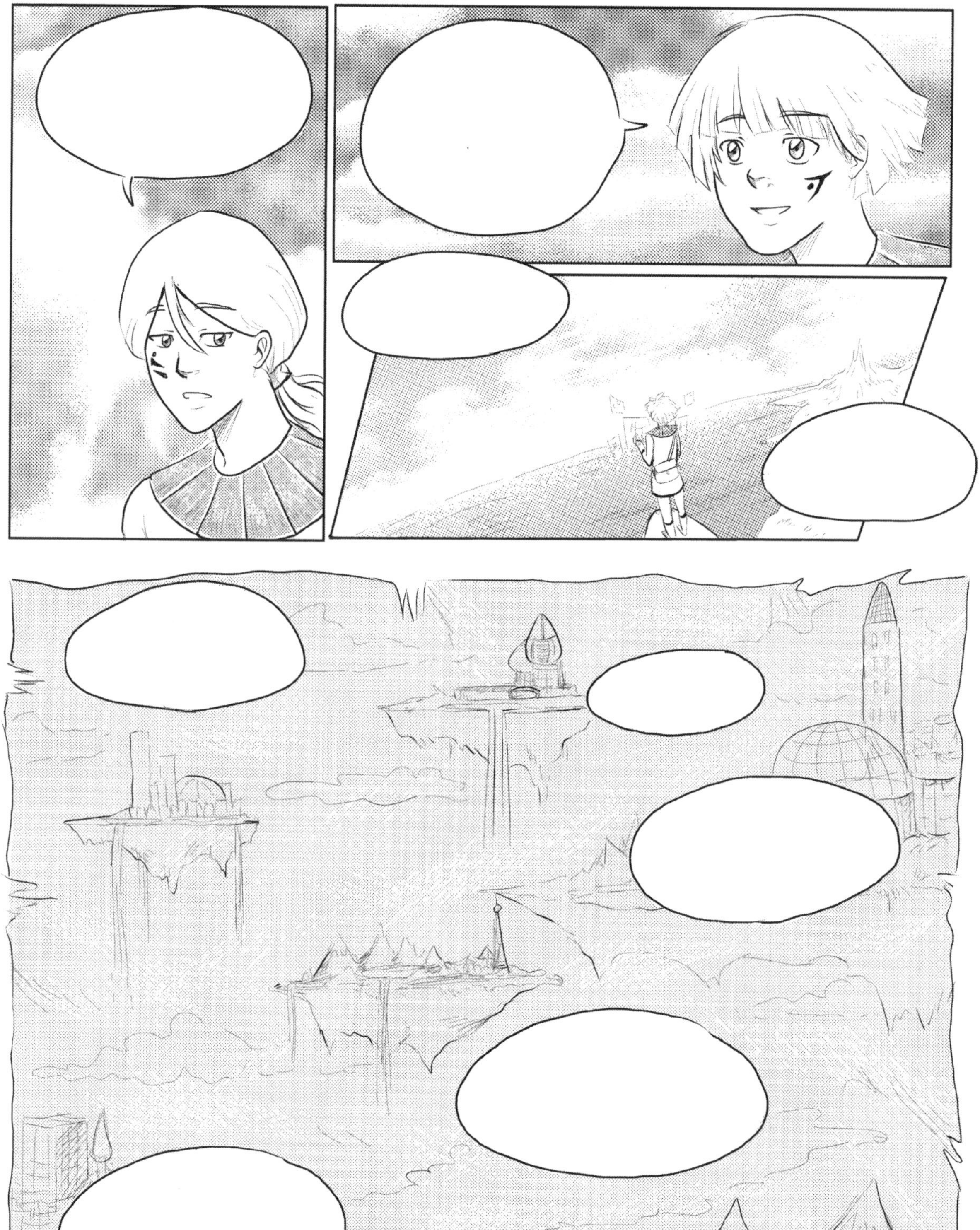

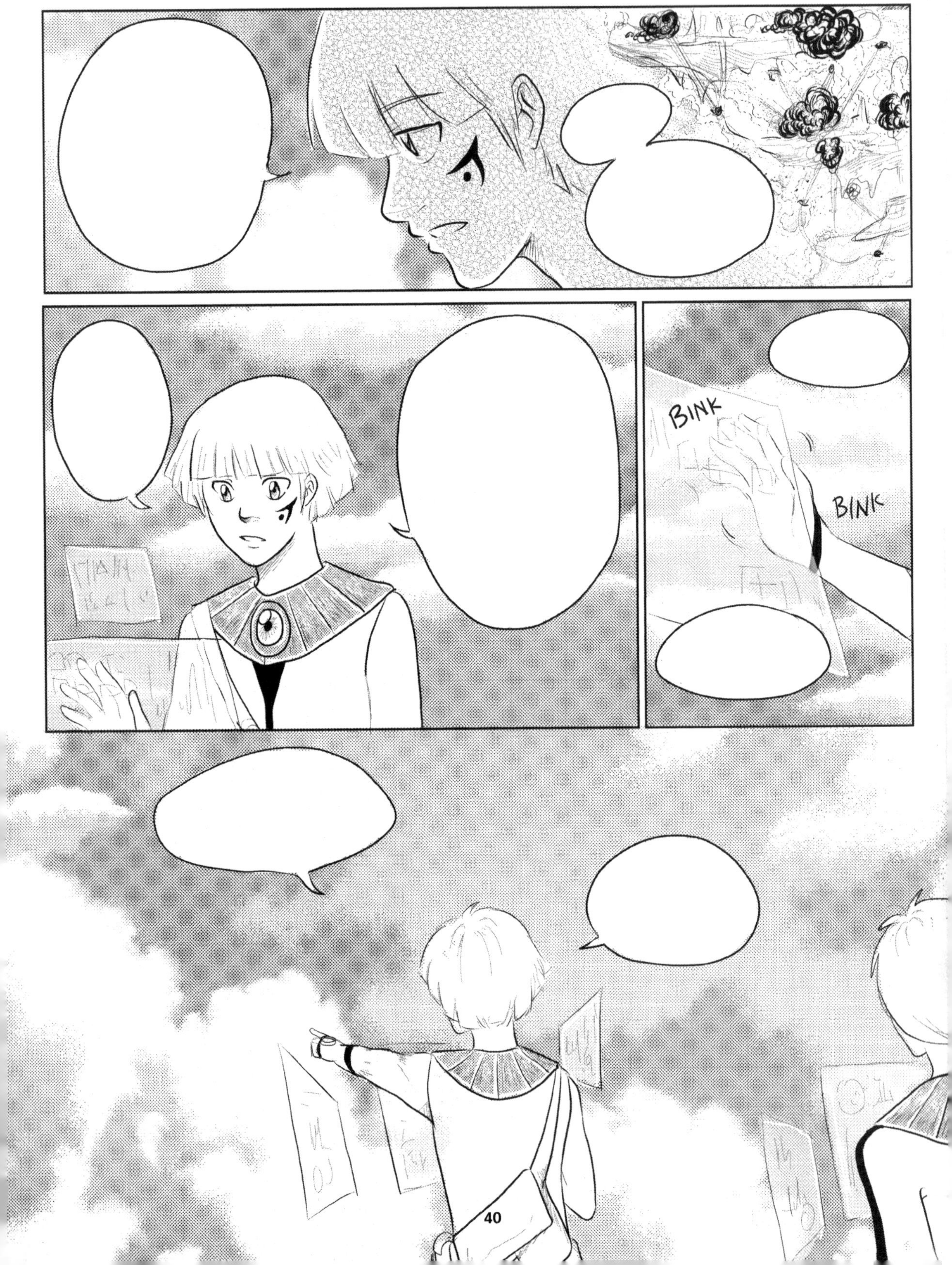
BINK
BINK

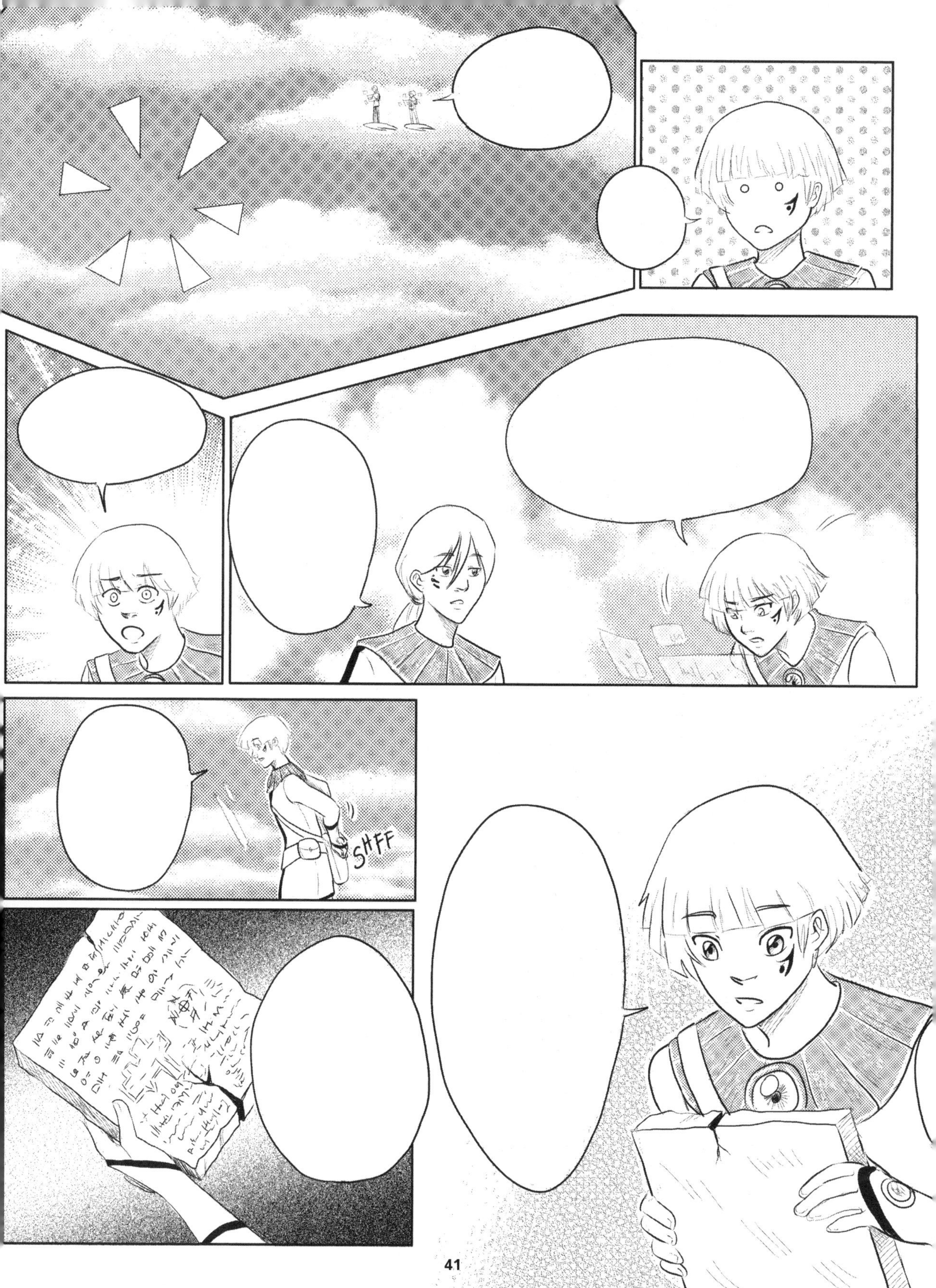
SHFF

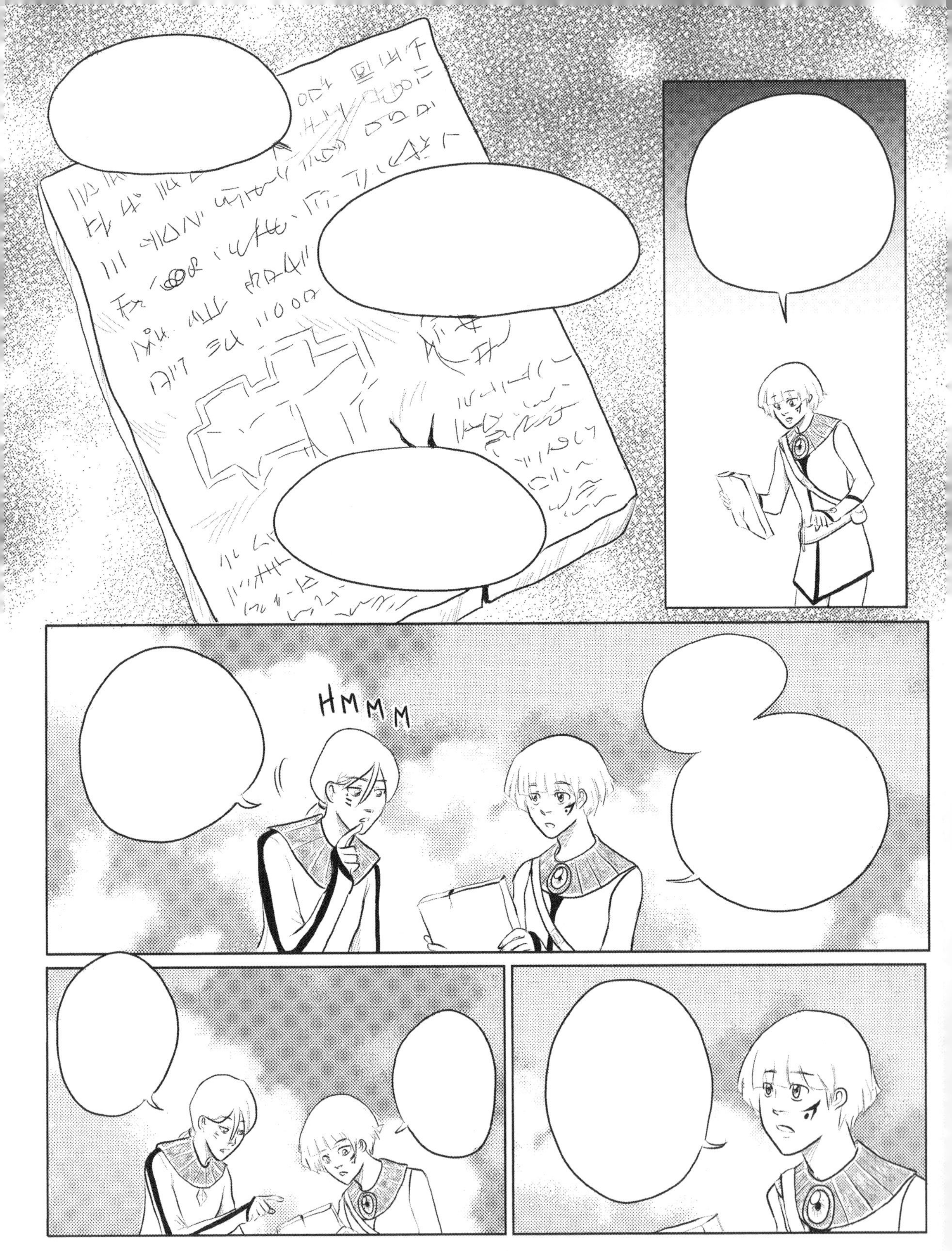
HMMM

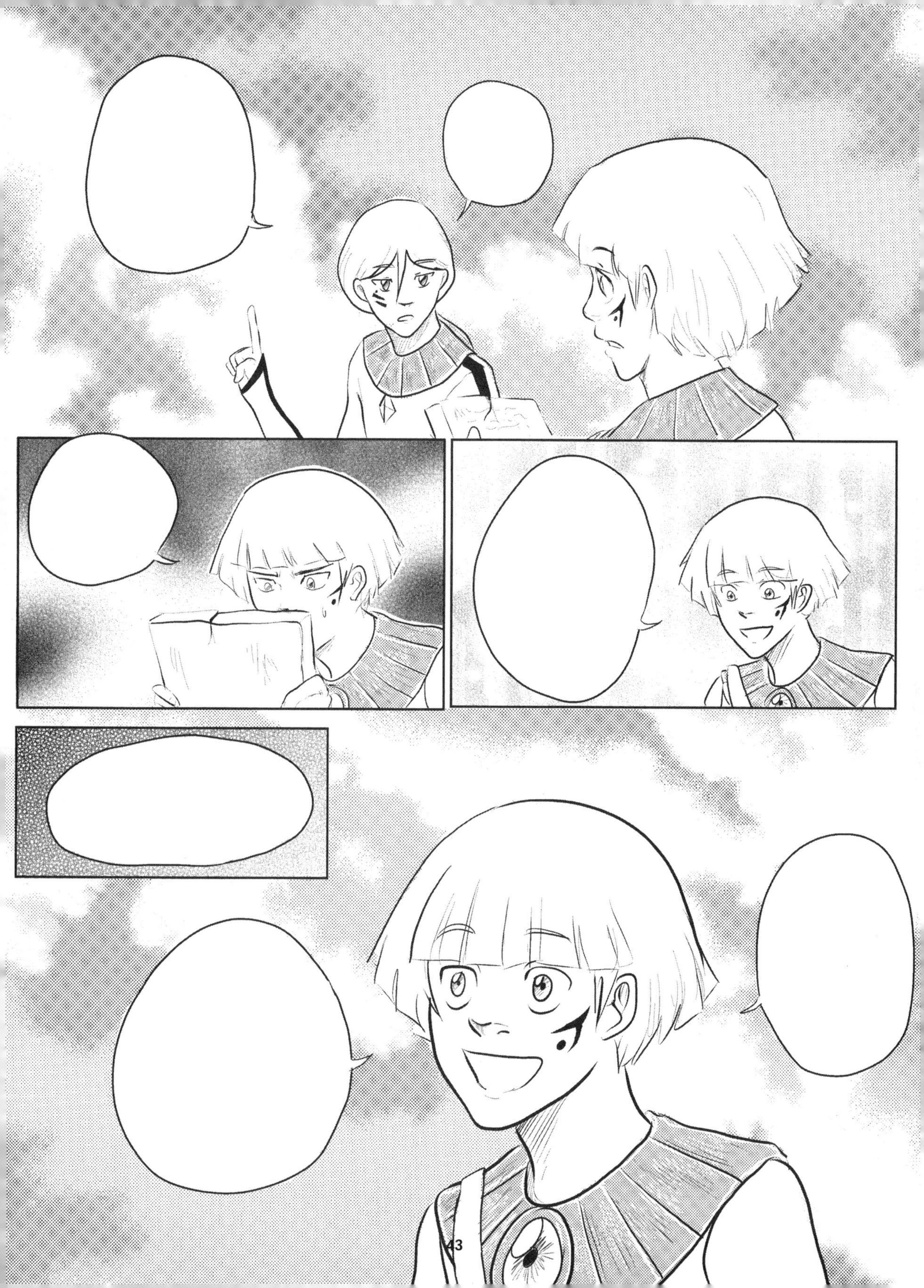

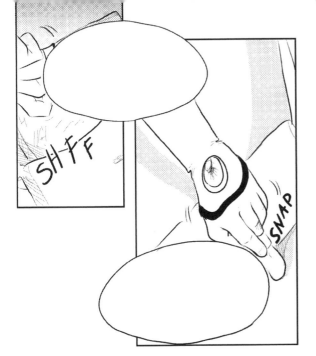

SHFF

SNAP

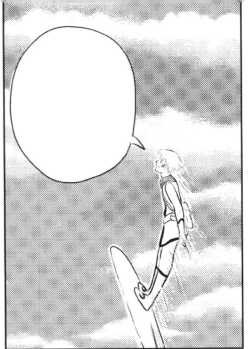

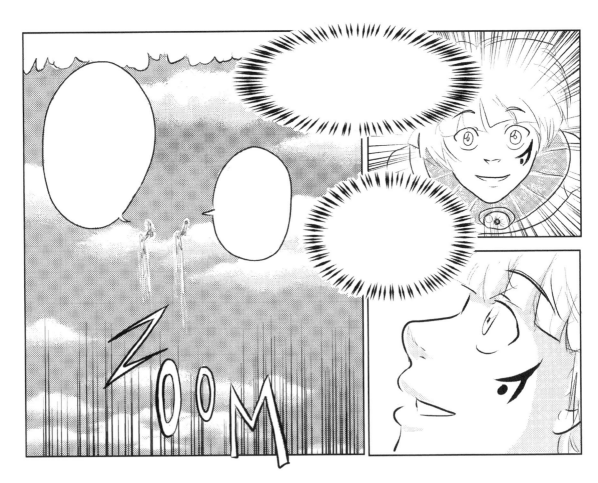

ZOOM

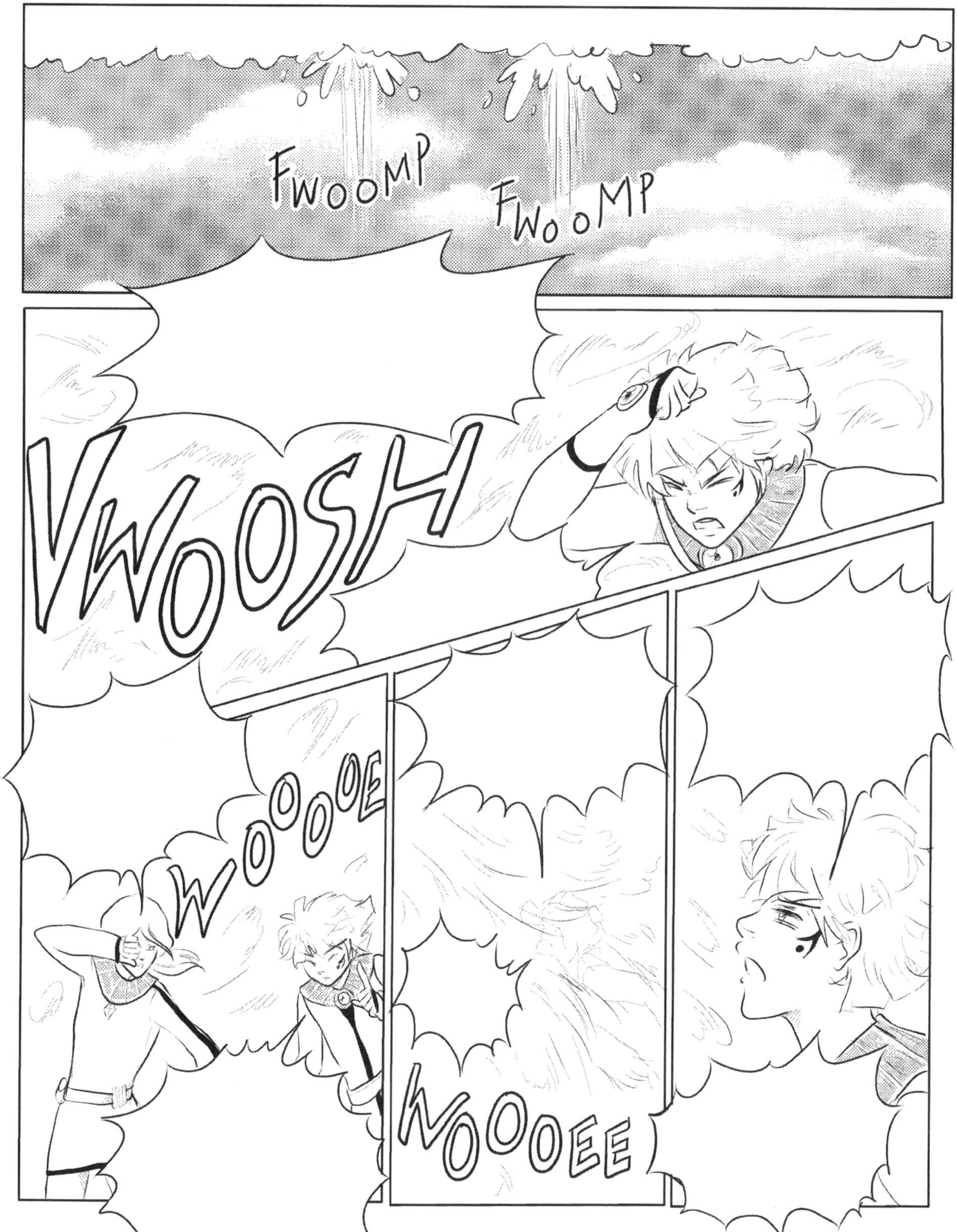
FWOOMP
FWOOMP
VWOOSH
WOOOOOE
WOOOEE

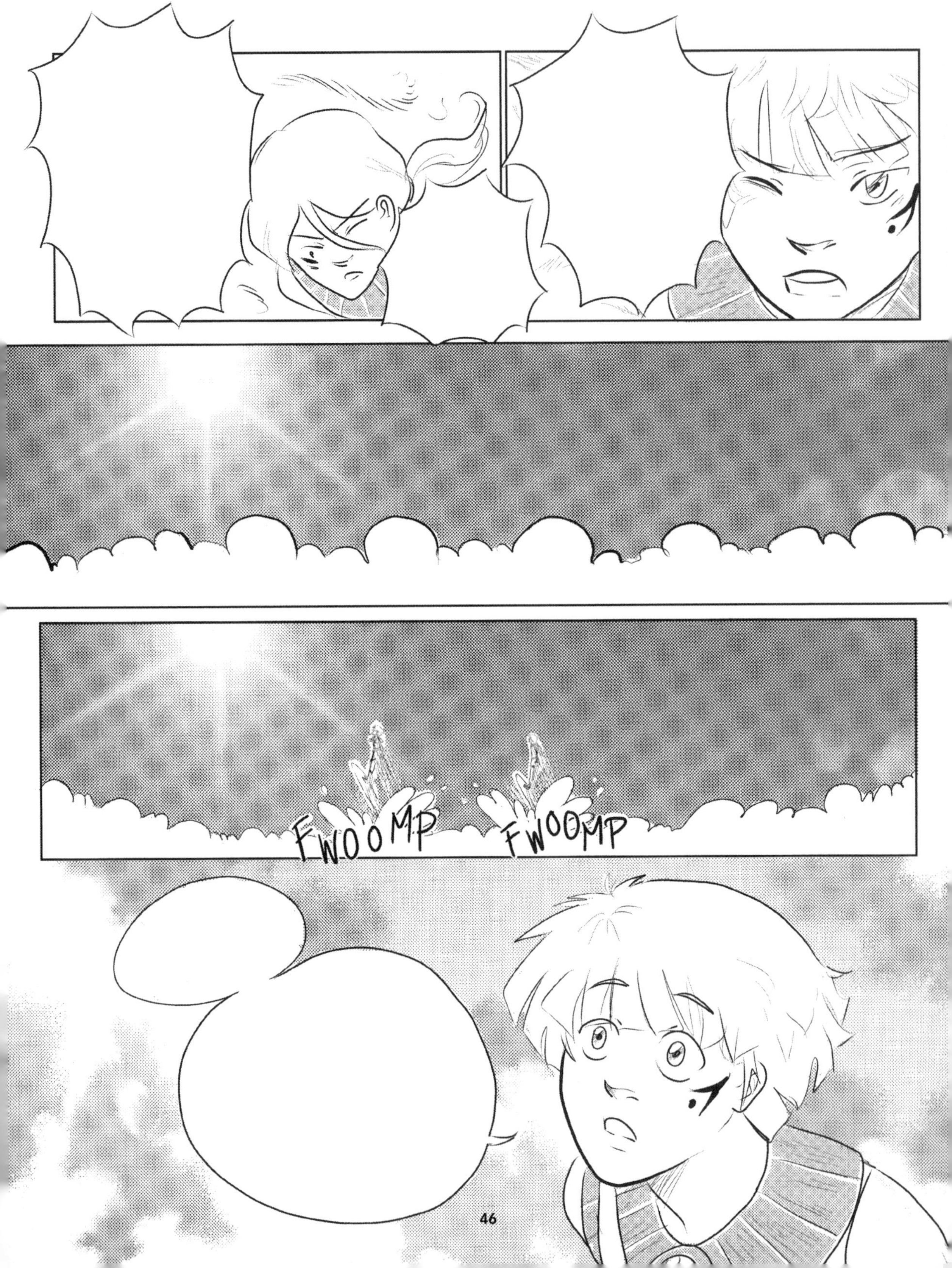
FWOOMP
FWOOMP

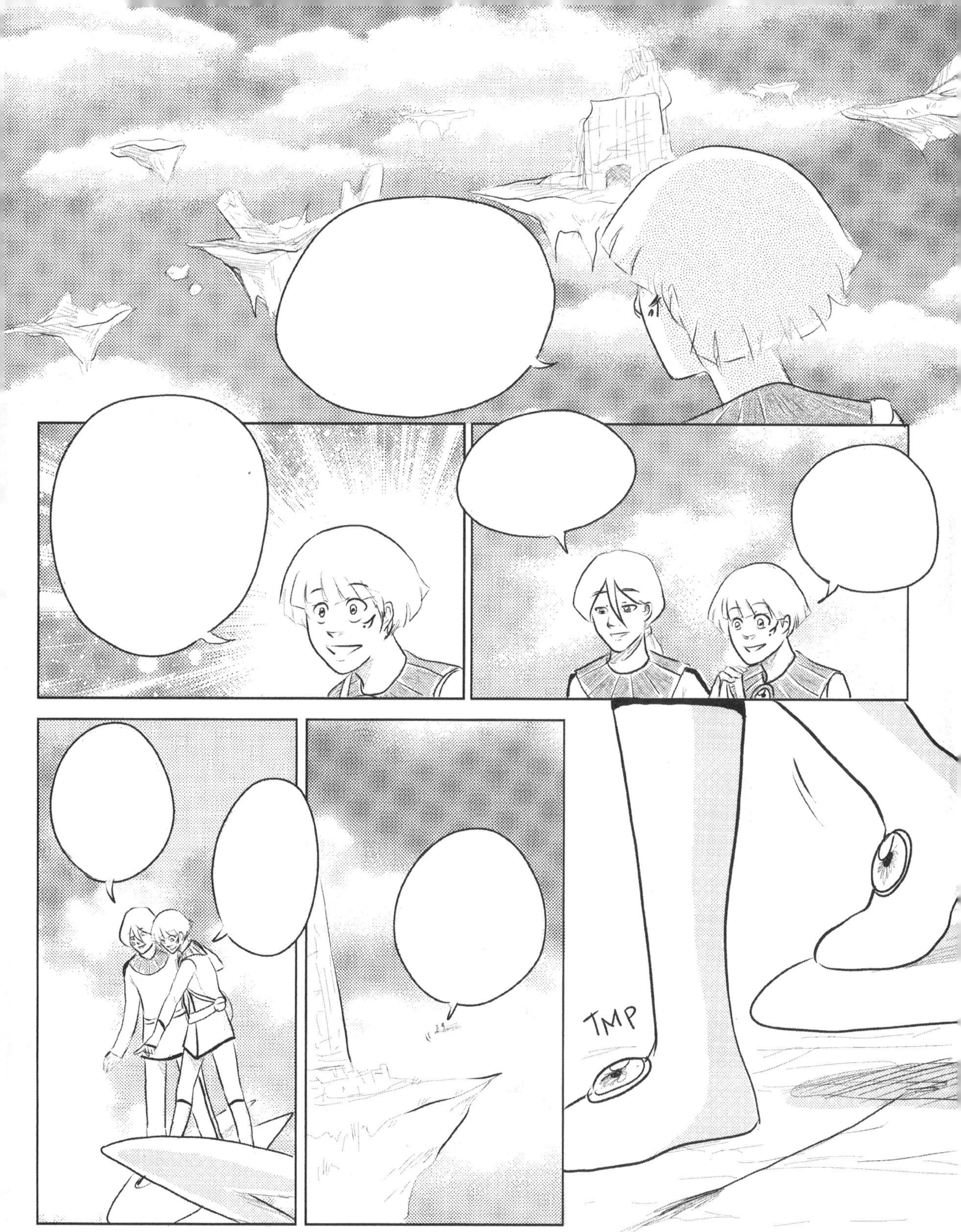
TMP

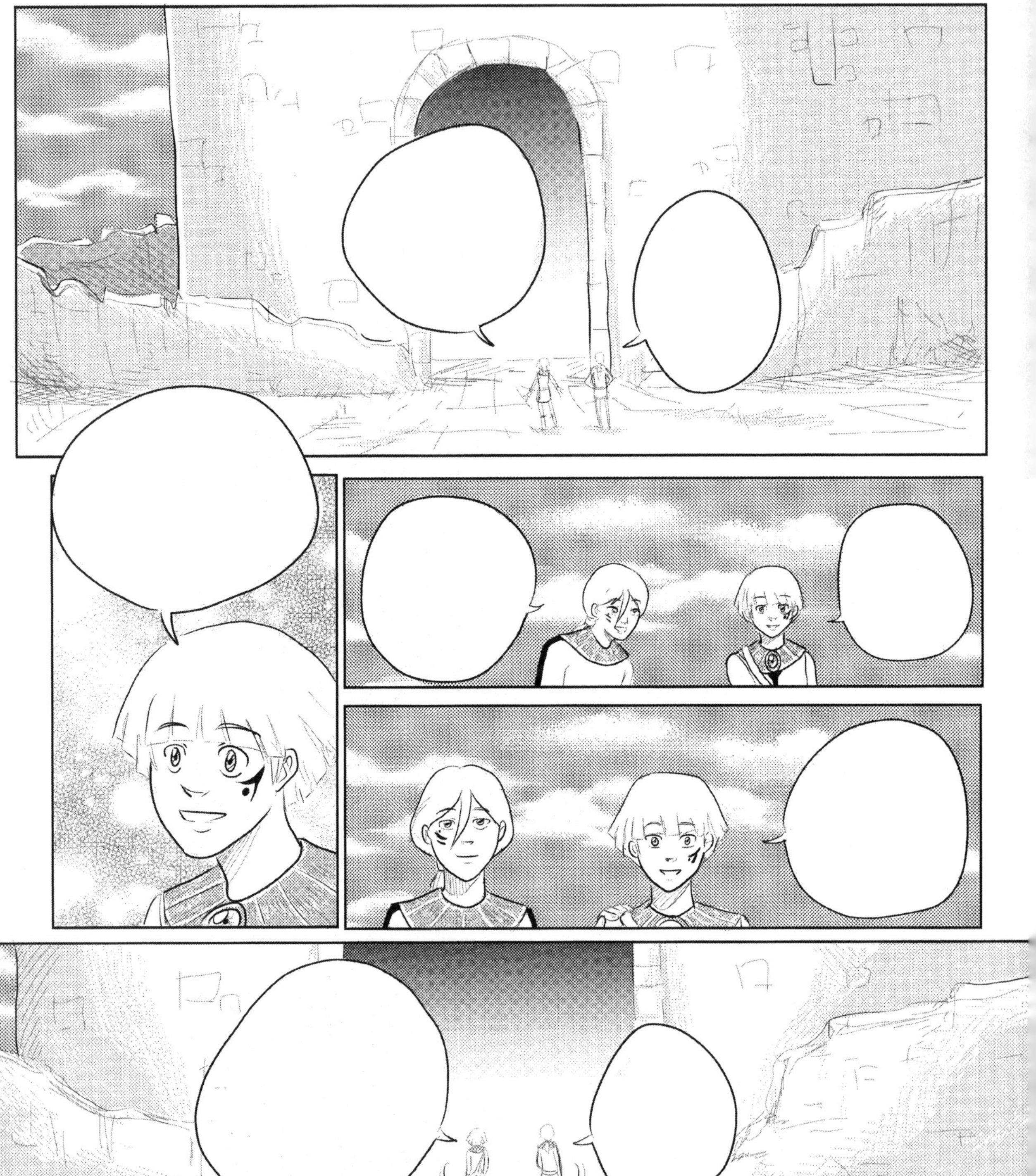
END

STORY #4

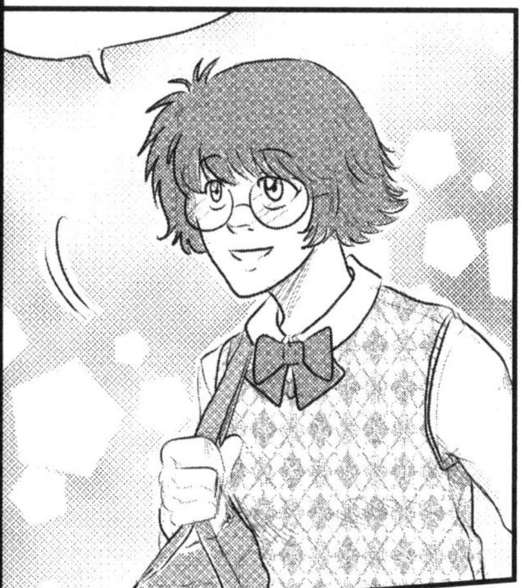

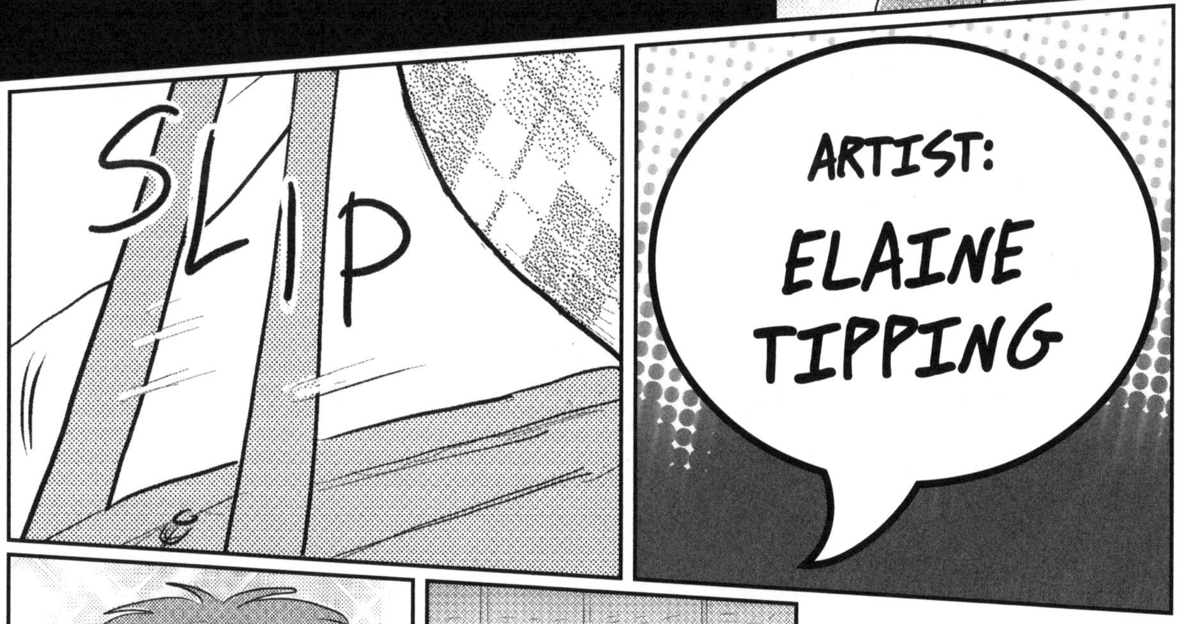
SLIP
ARTIST:
ELAINE TIPPING

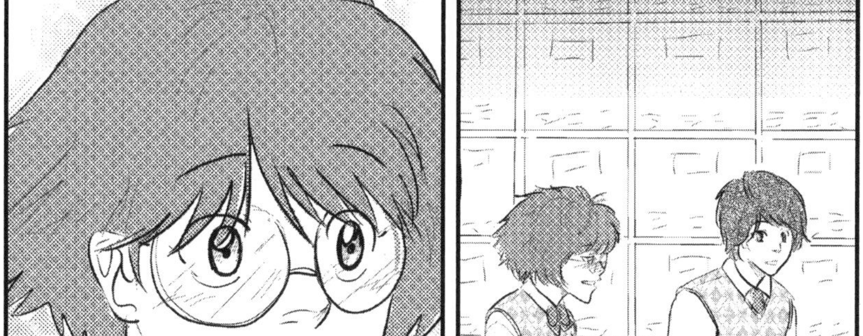

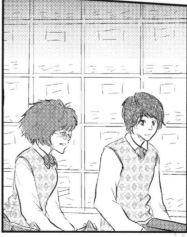

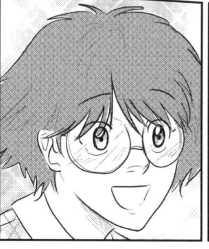

TITLE:

____

____

____

WRITER:

____

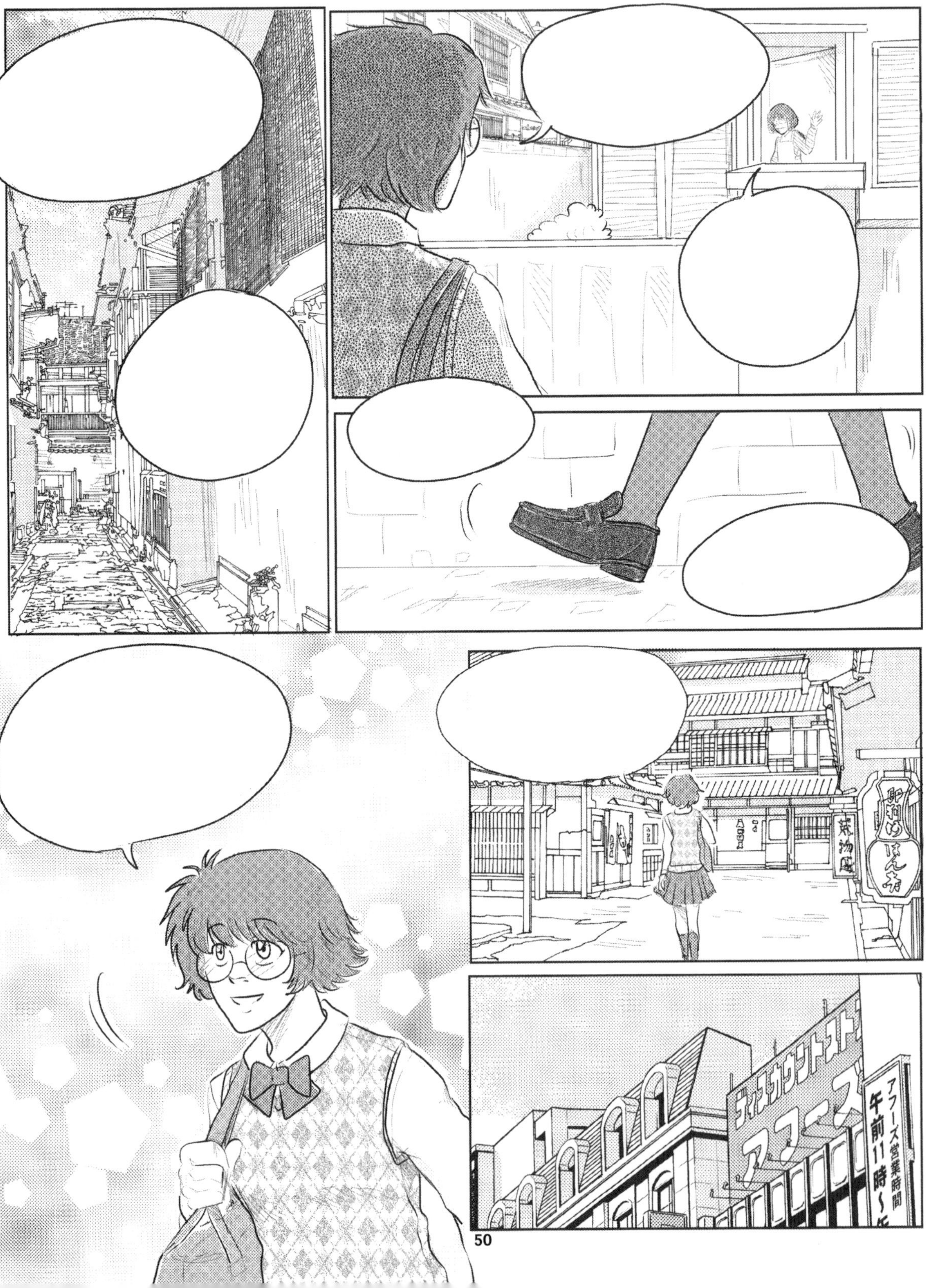
アフーズ営業時間
午前11時〜

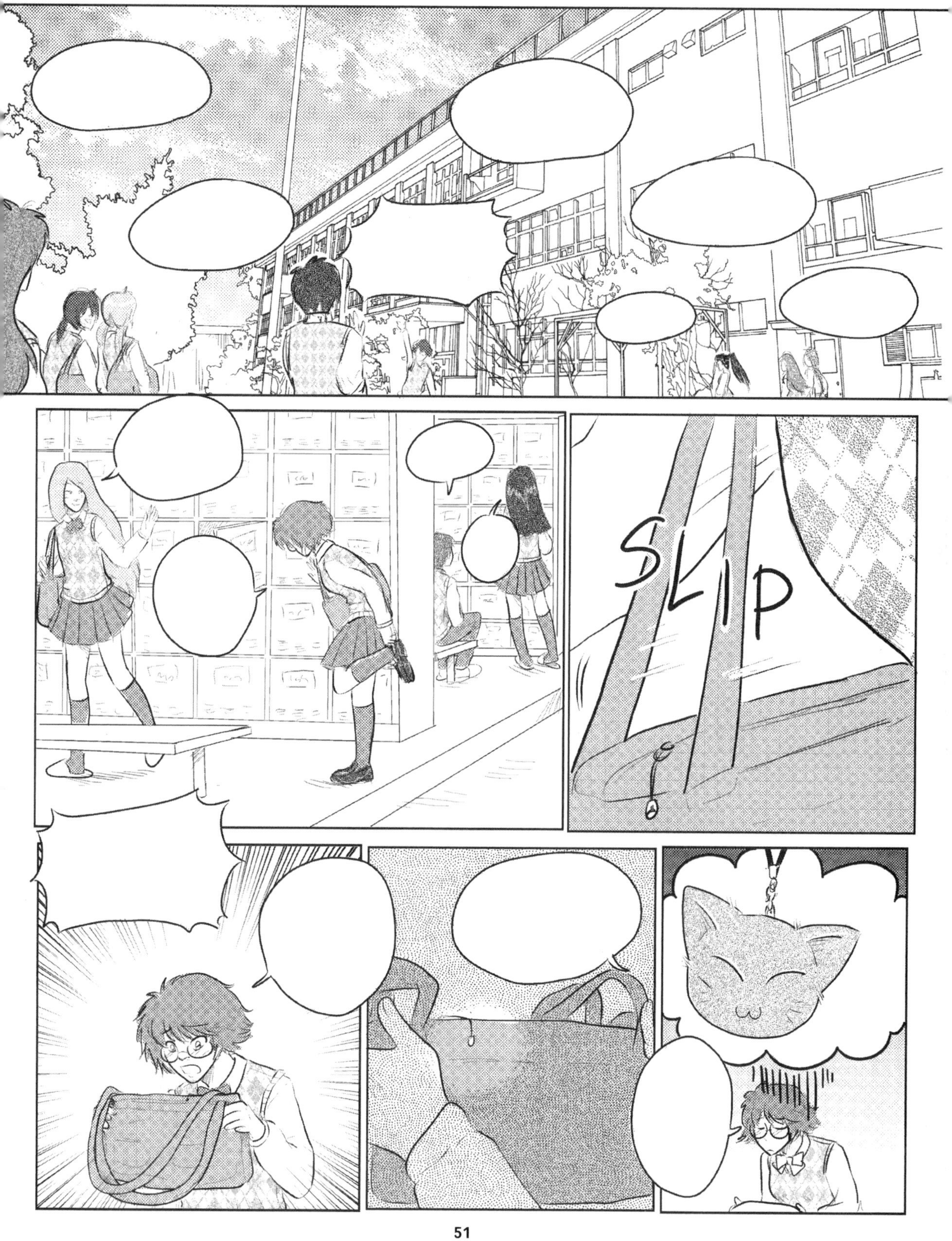
SLIP

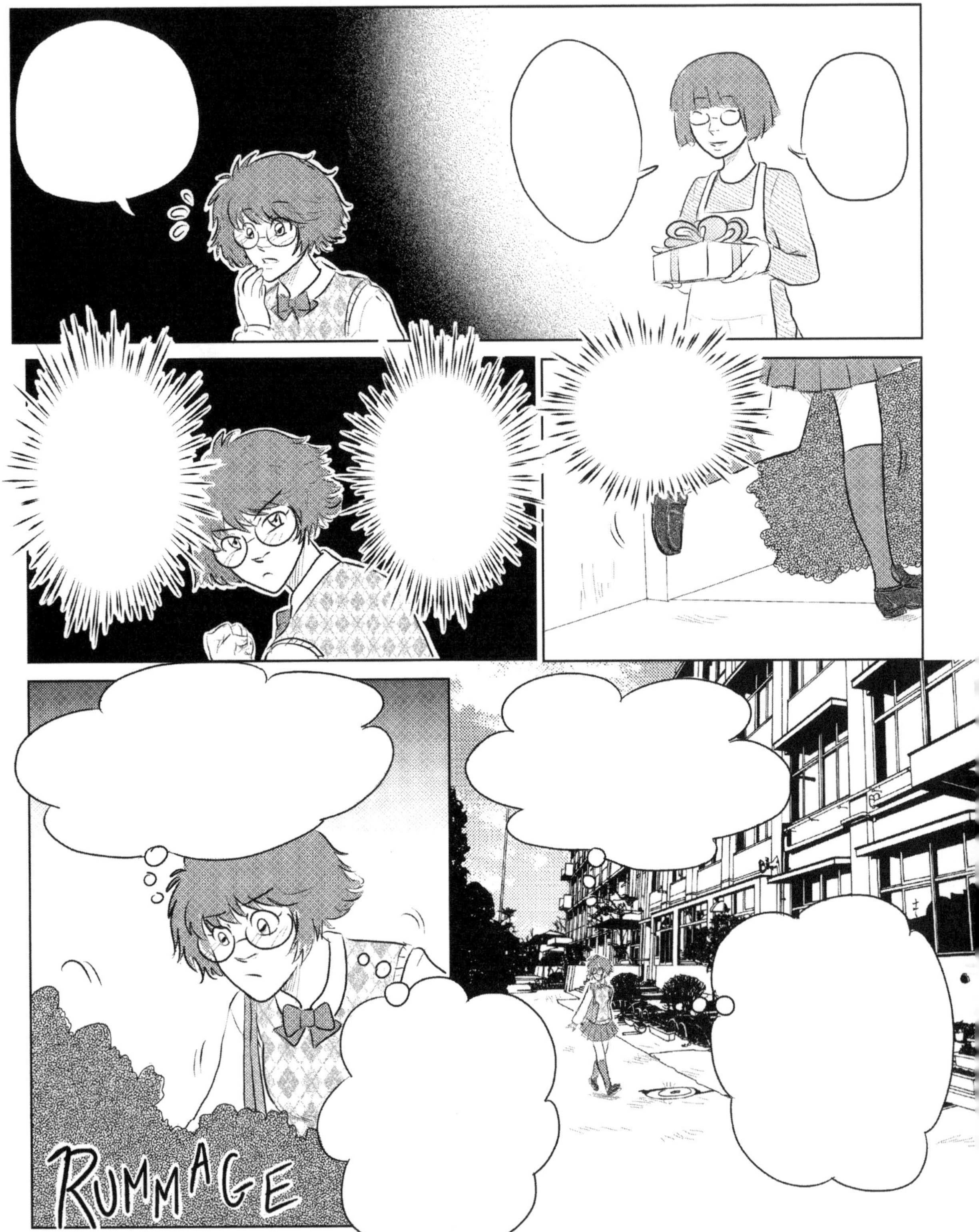
RUMMAGE

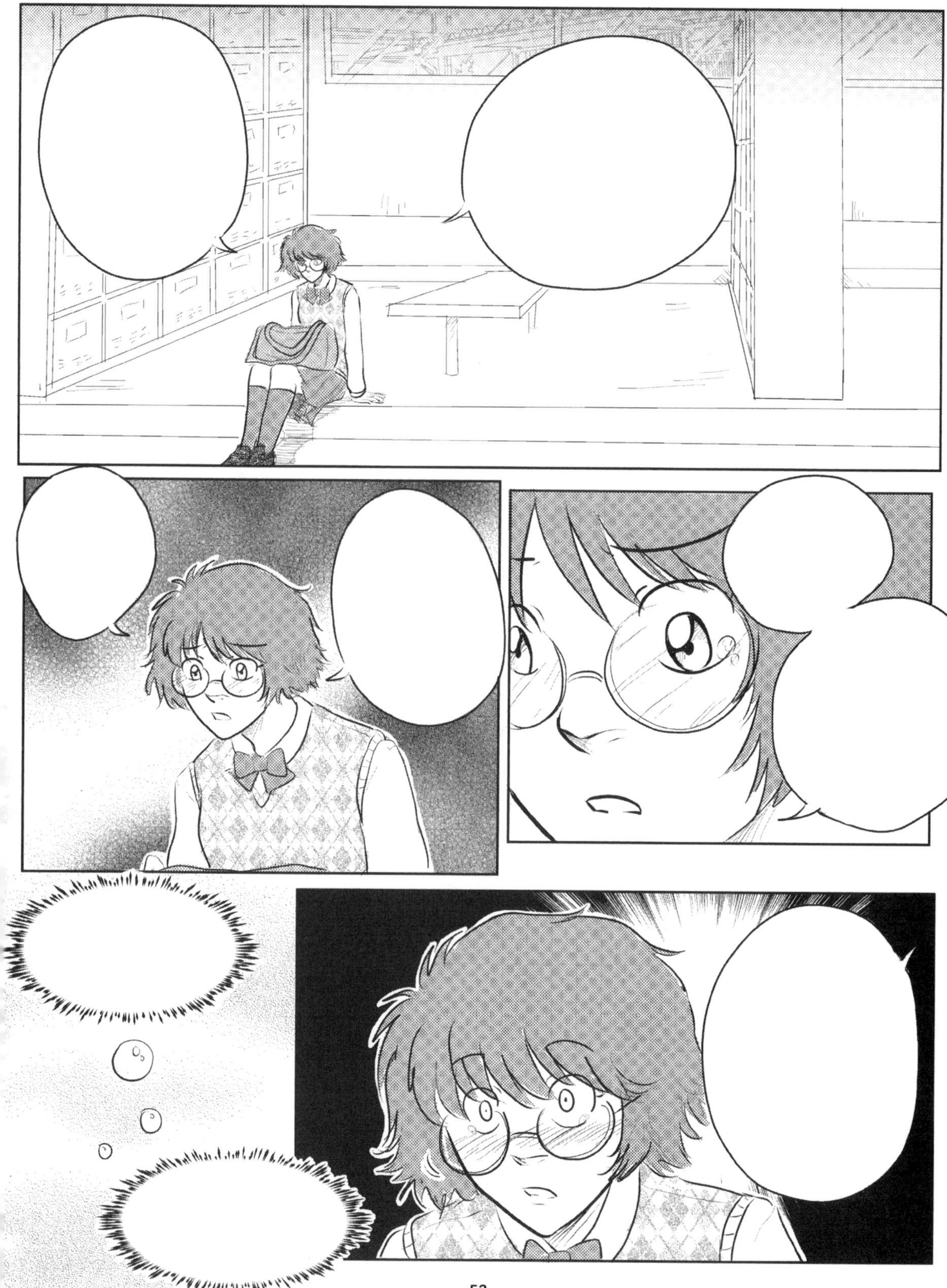

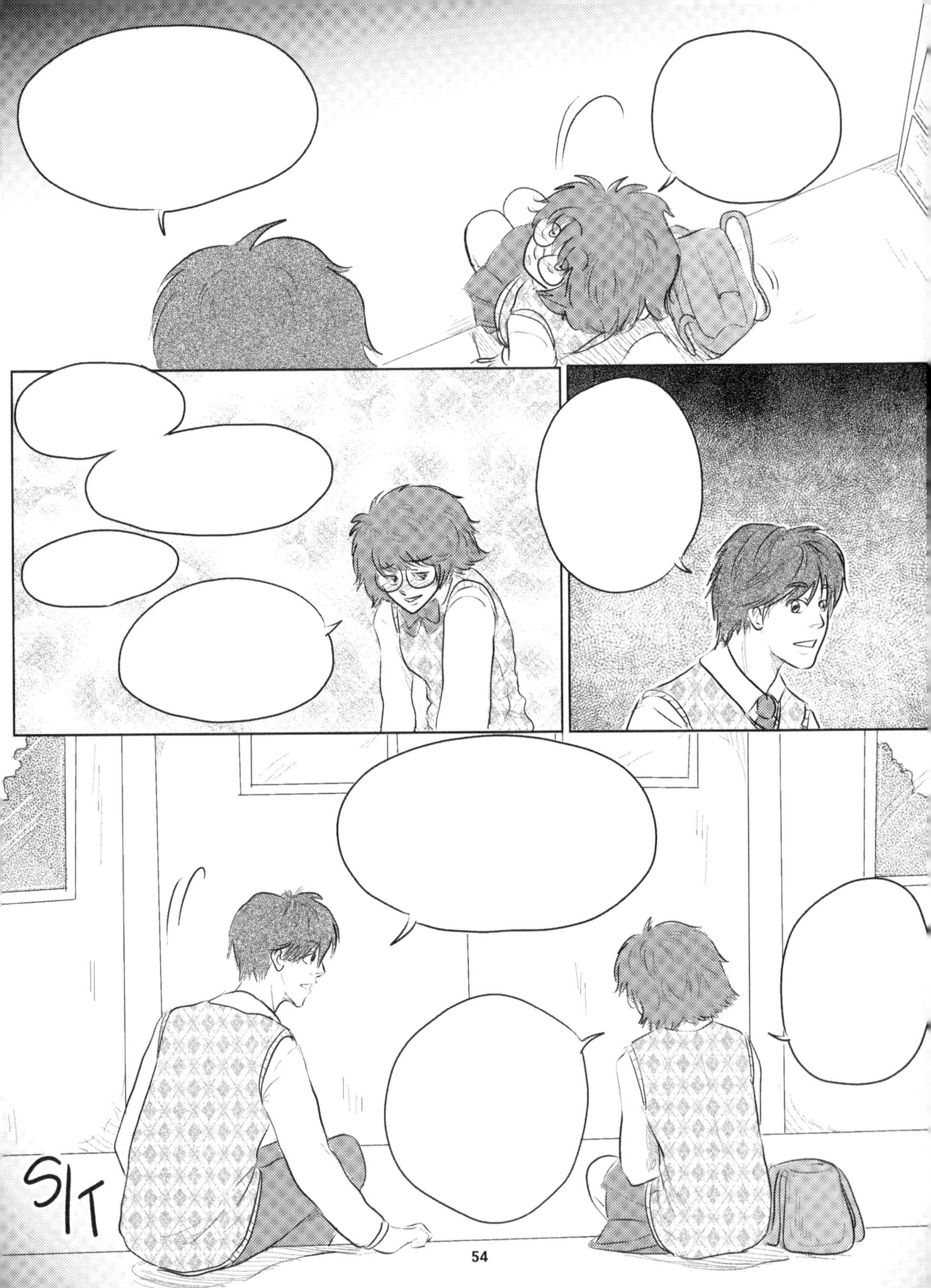
SIT

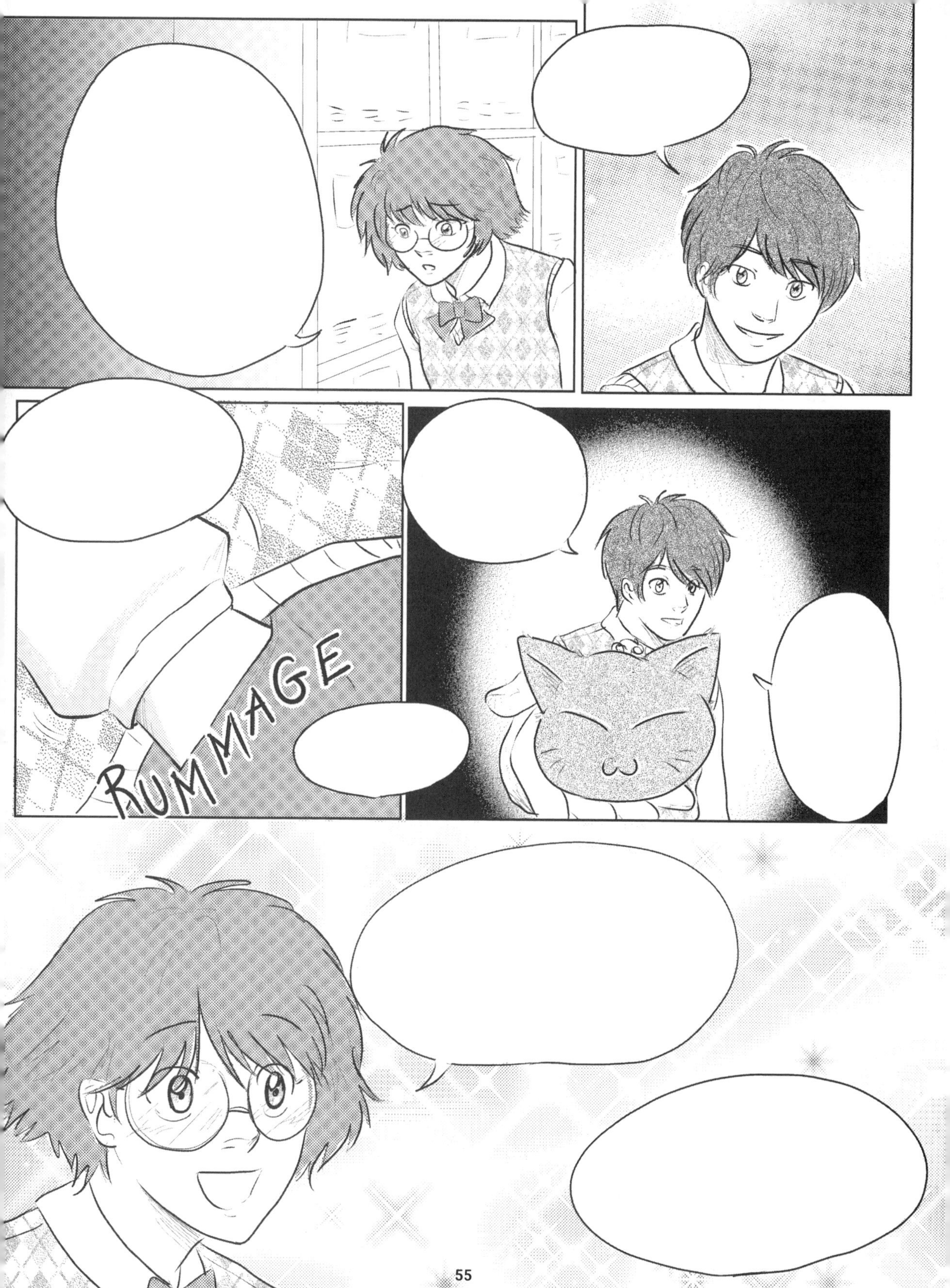
RUMMAGE

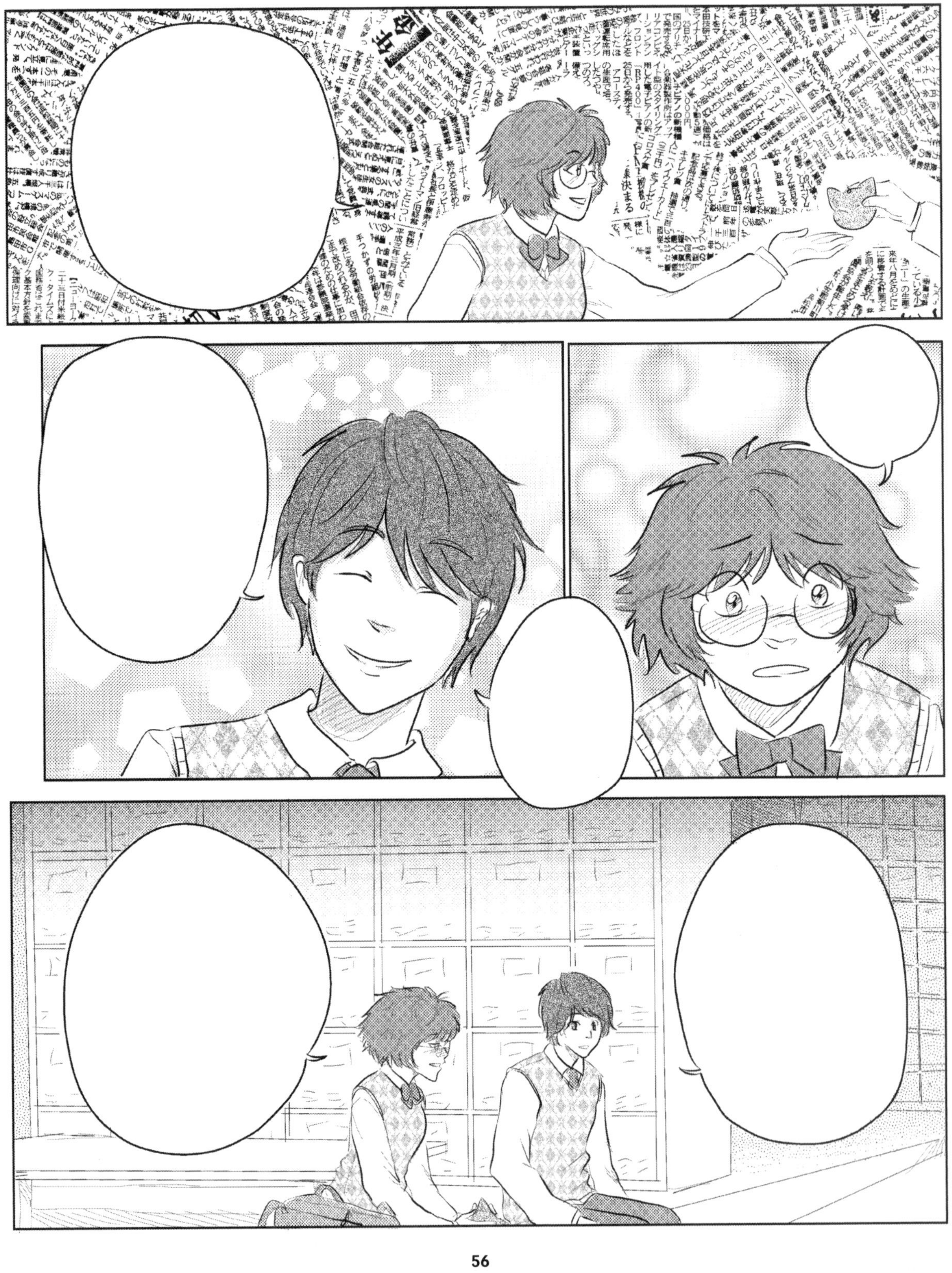

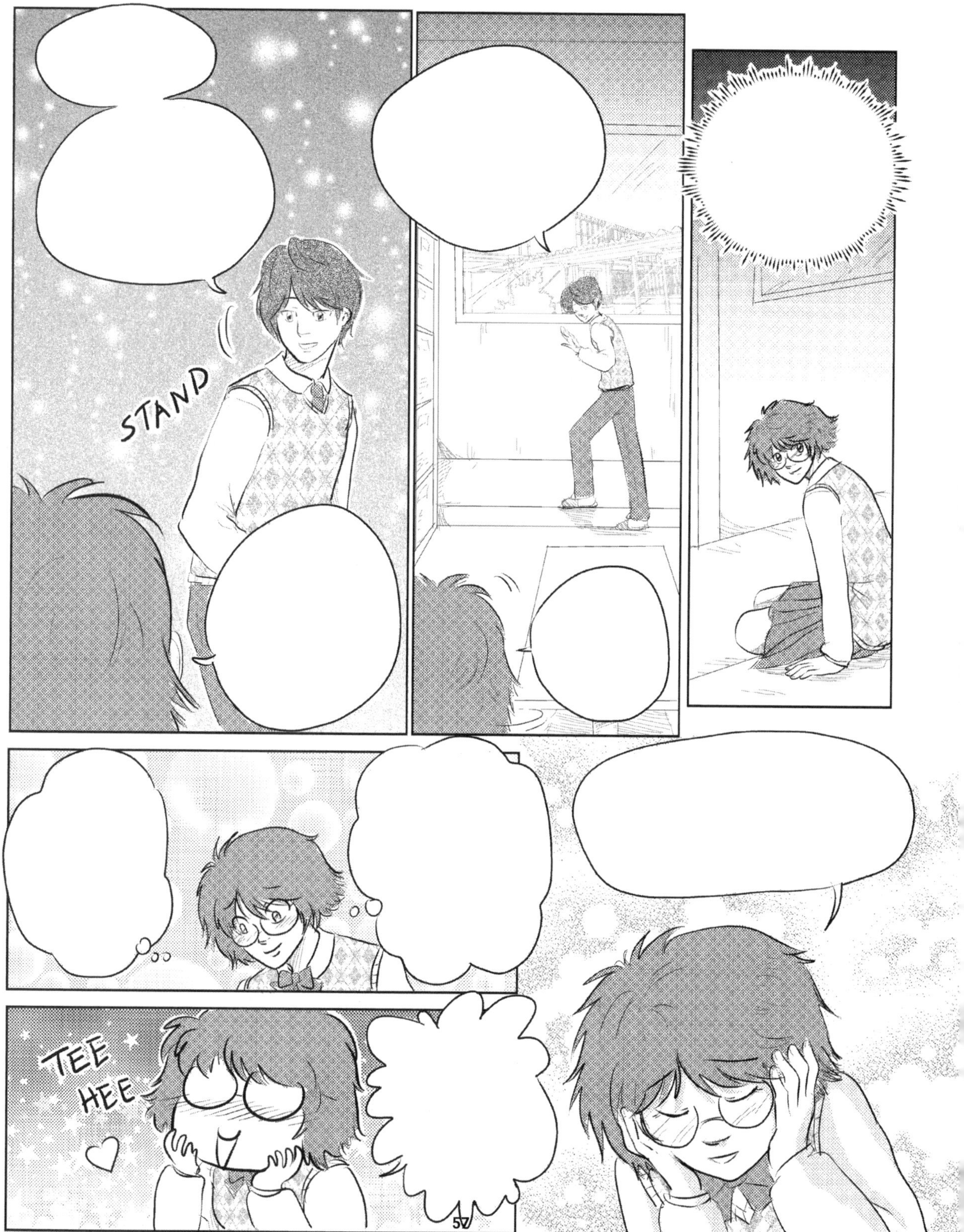
STAND
TEE HEE

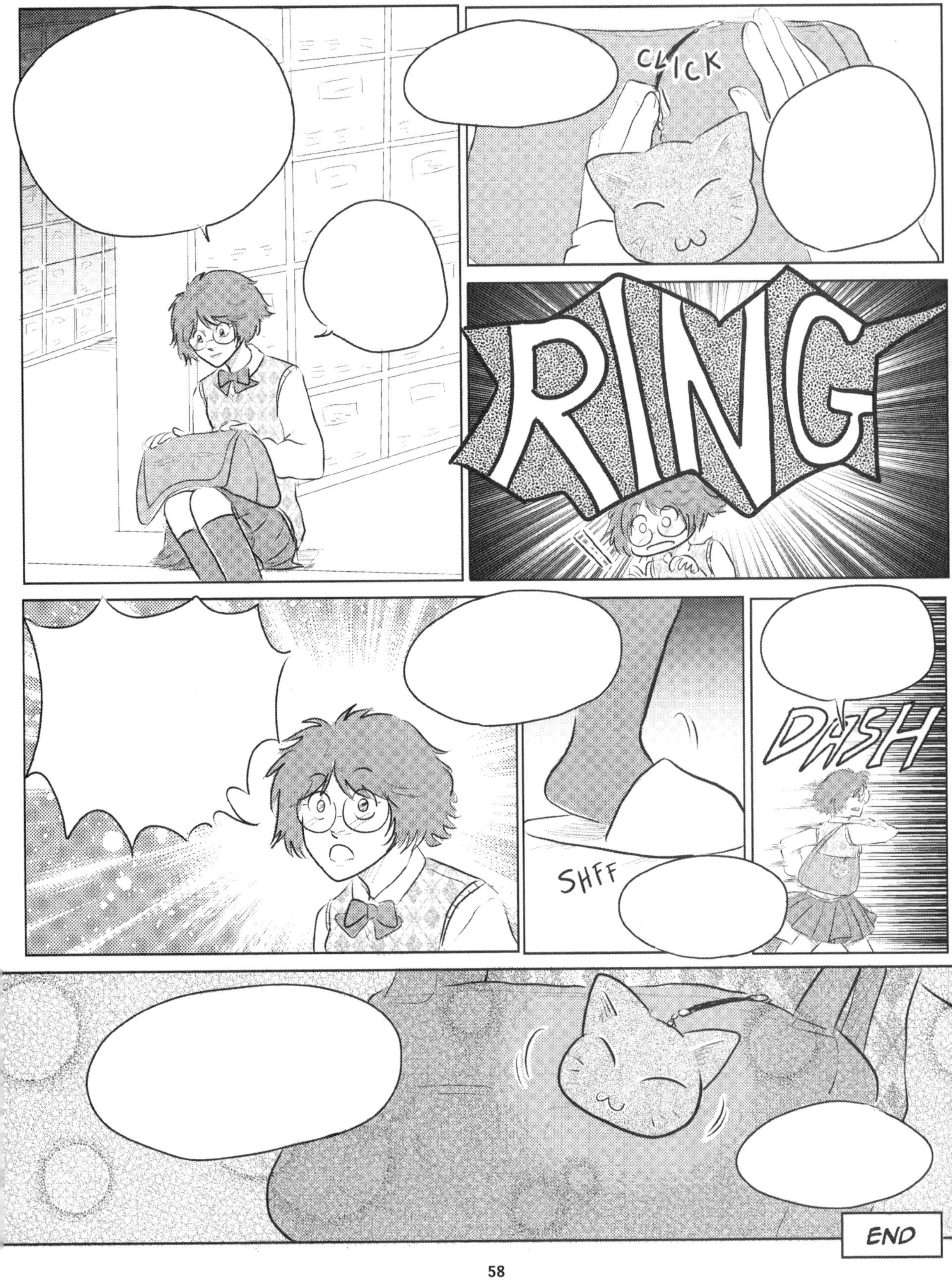
CLICK
RING
DASH
SHFF
END

STORY #5

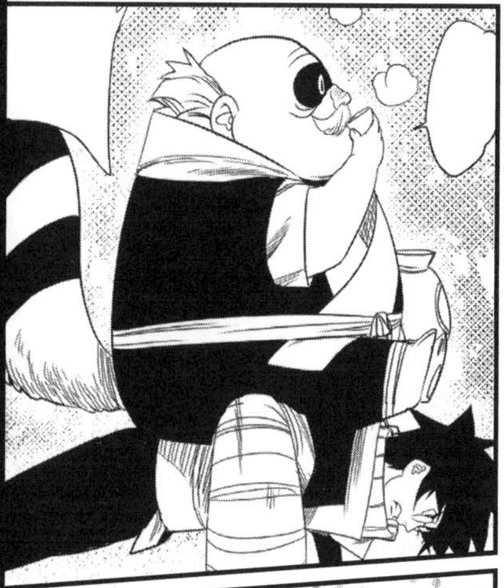

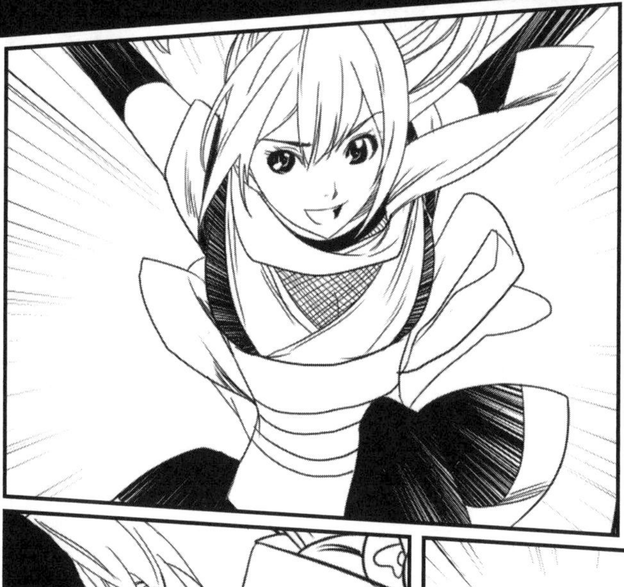

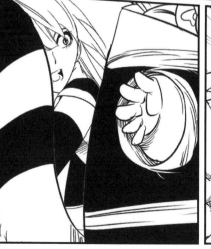

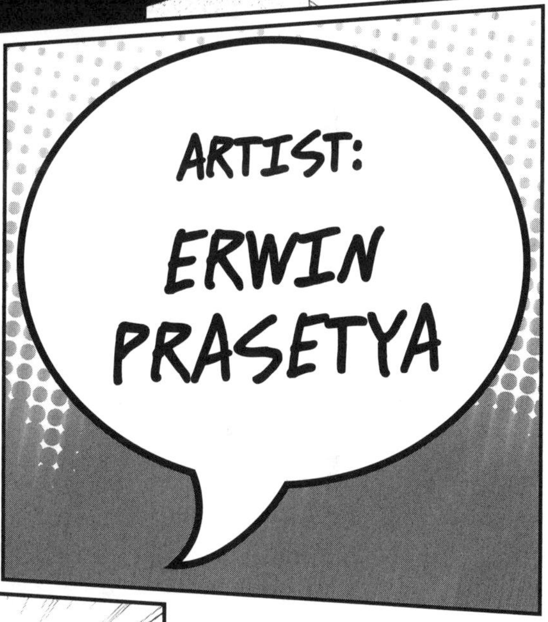
ARTIST:
ERWIN PRASETYA

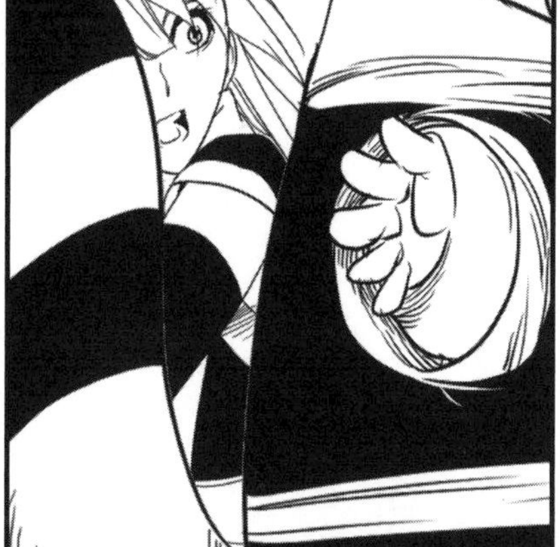

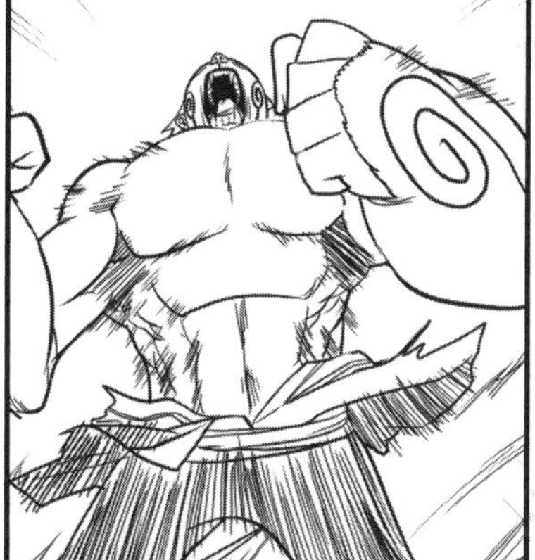

TITLE:

____

____

____

WRITER:

____

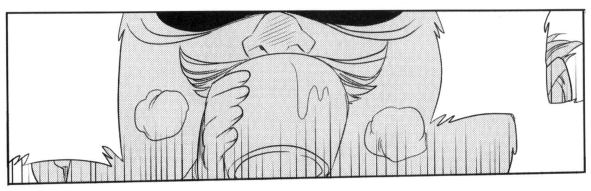

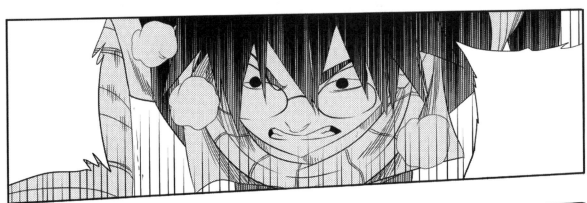

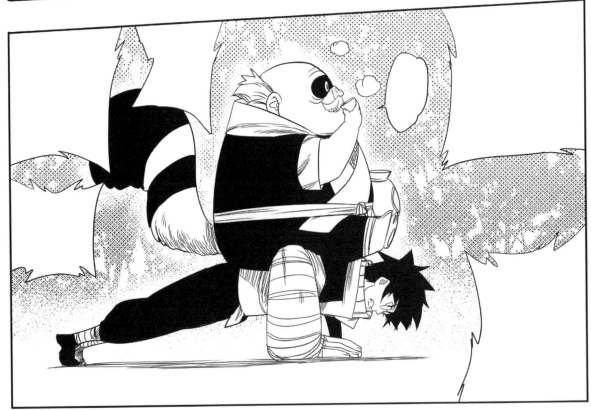

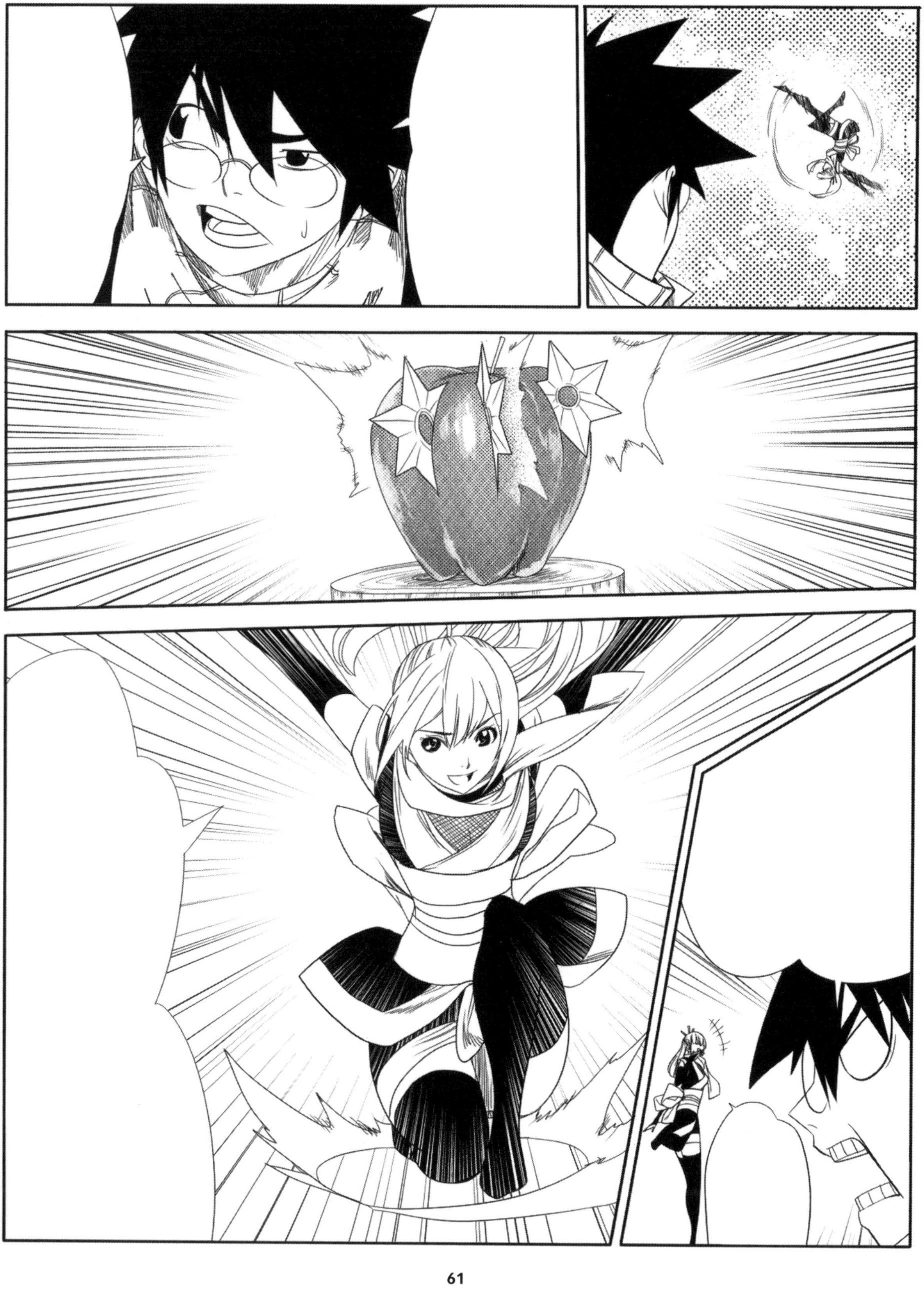

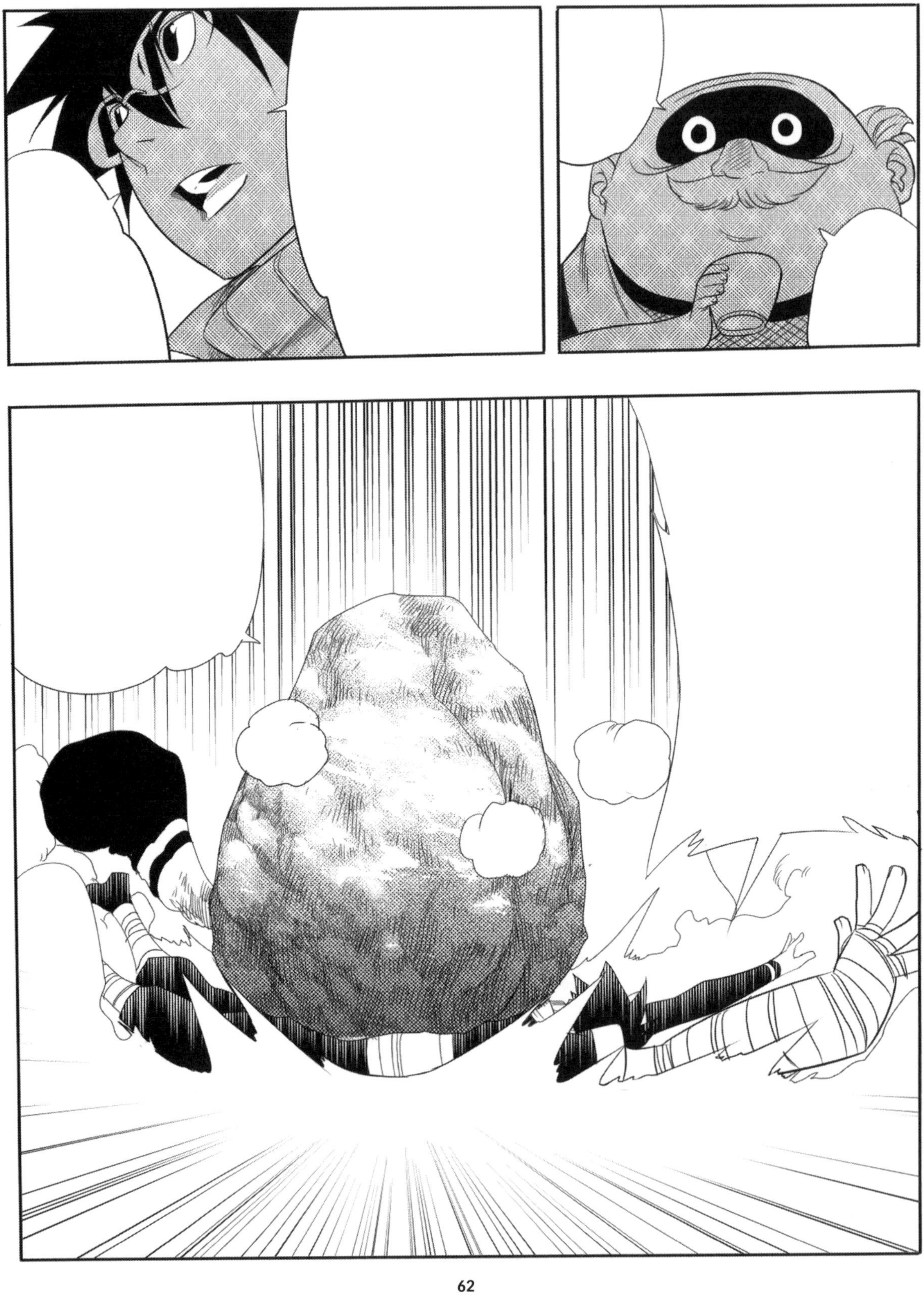

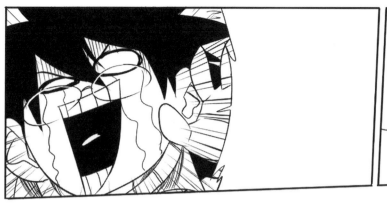
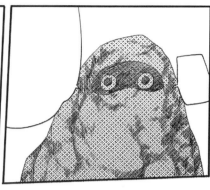
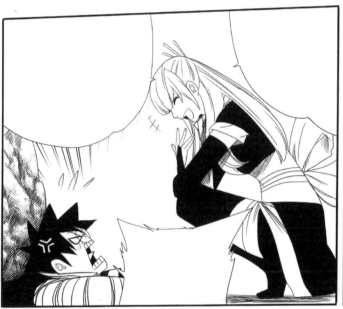
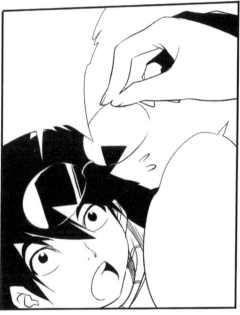
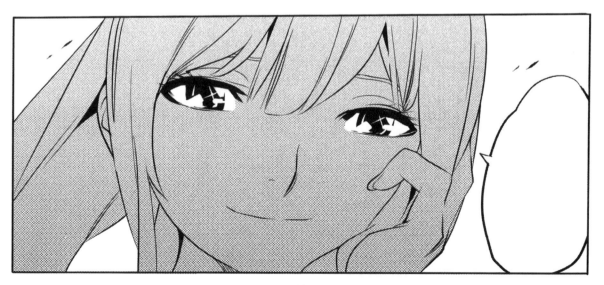

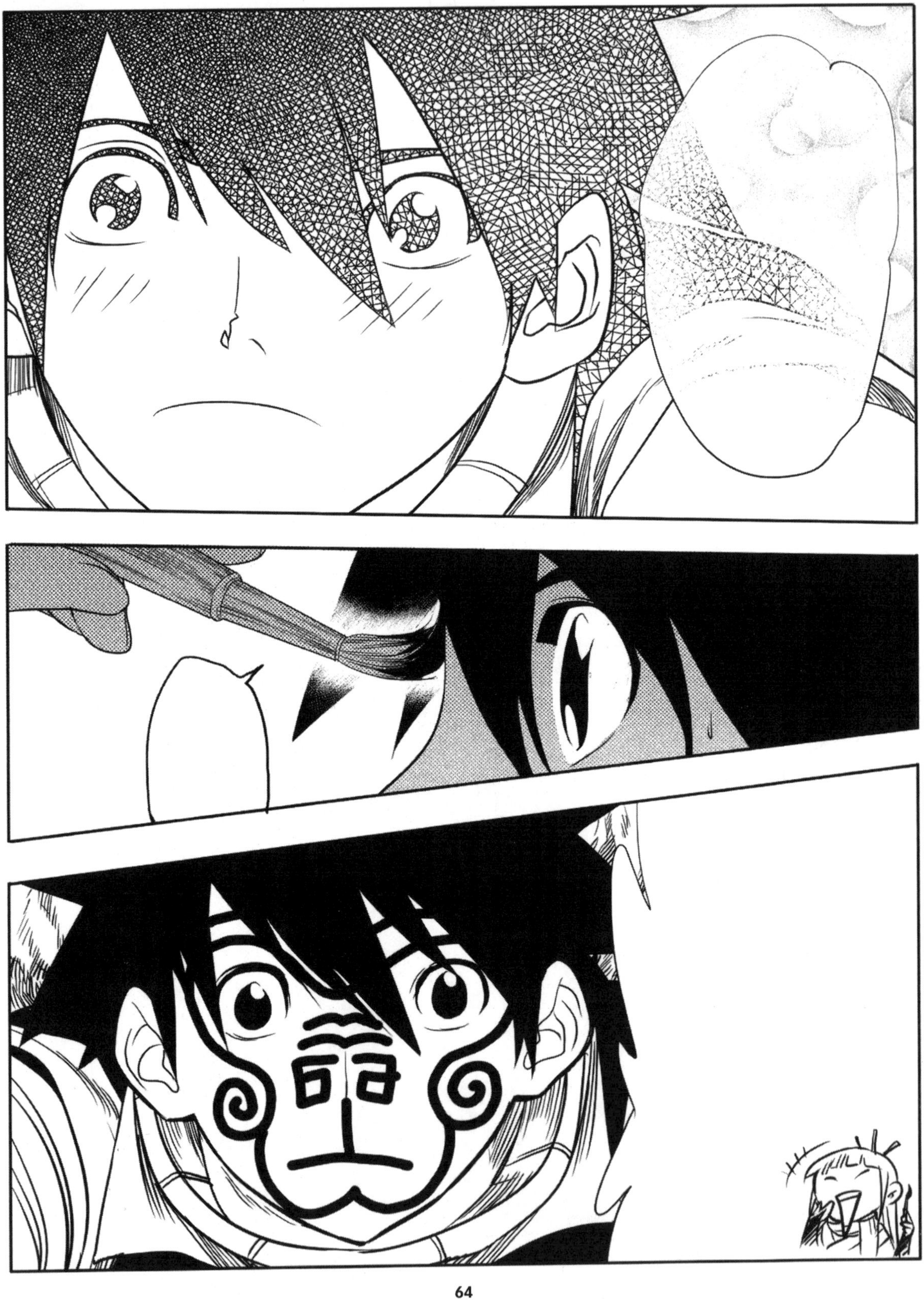

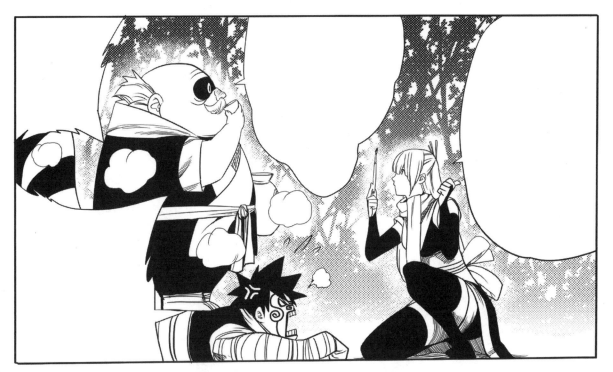

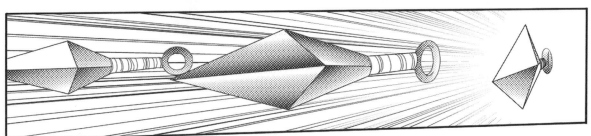

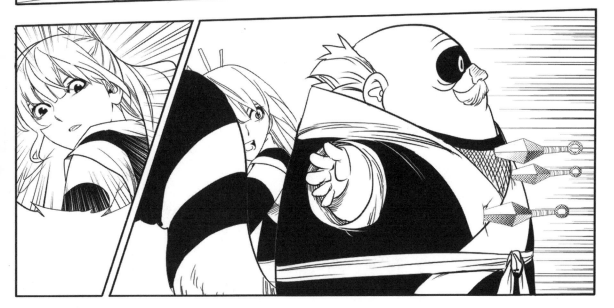

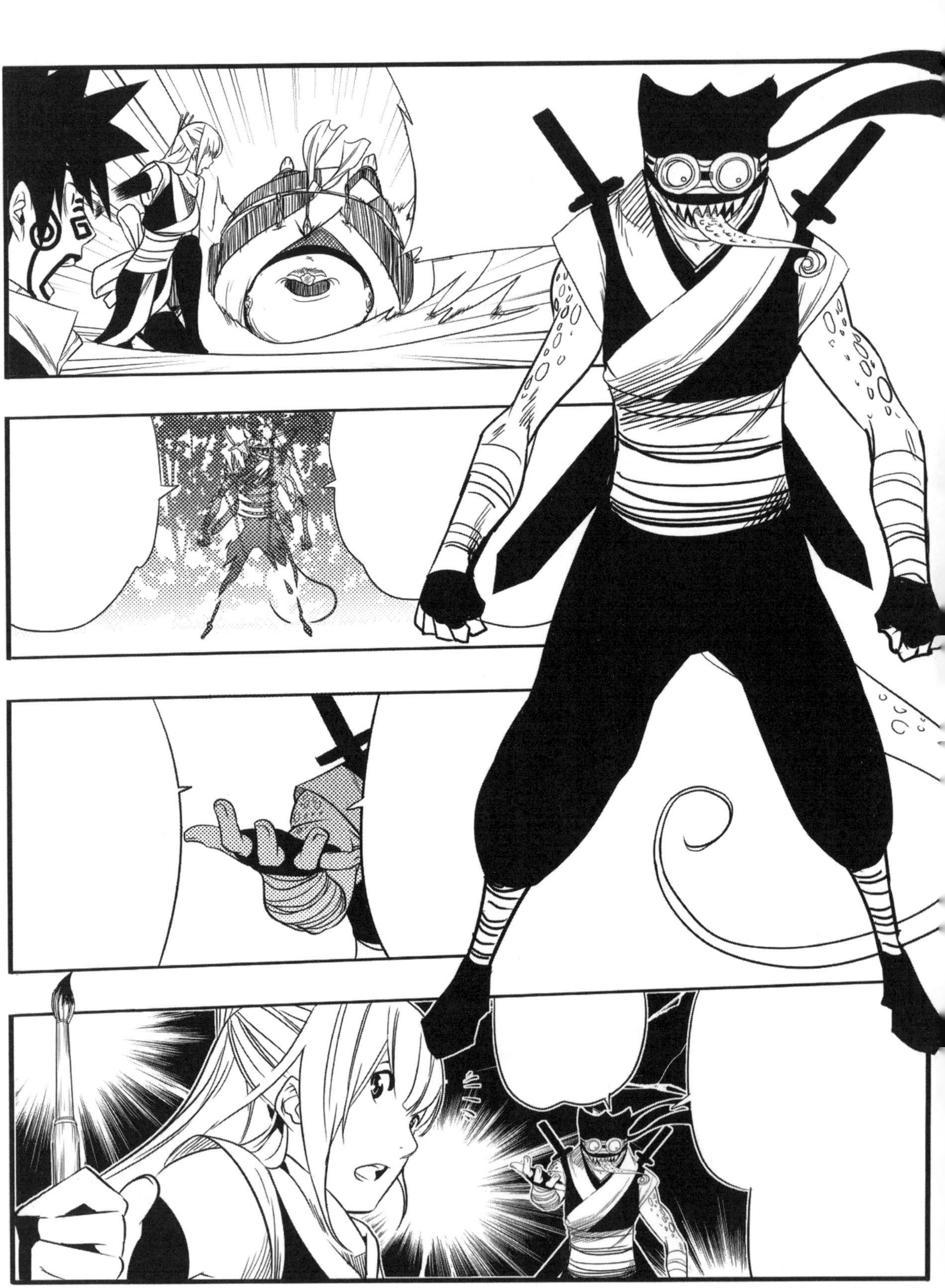

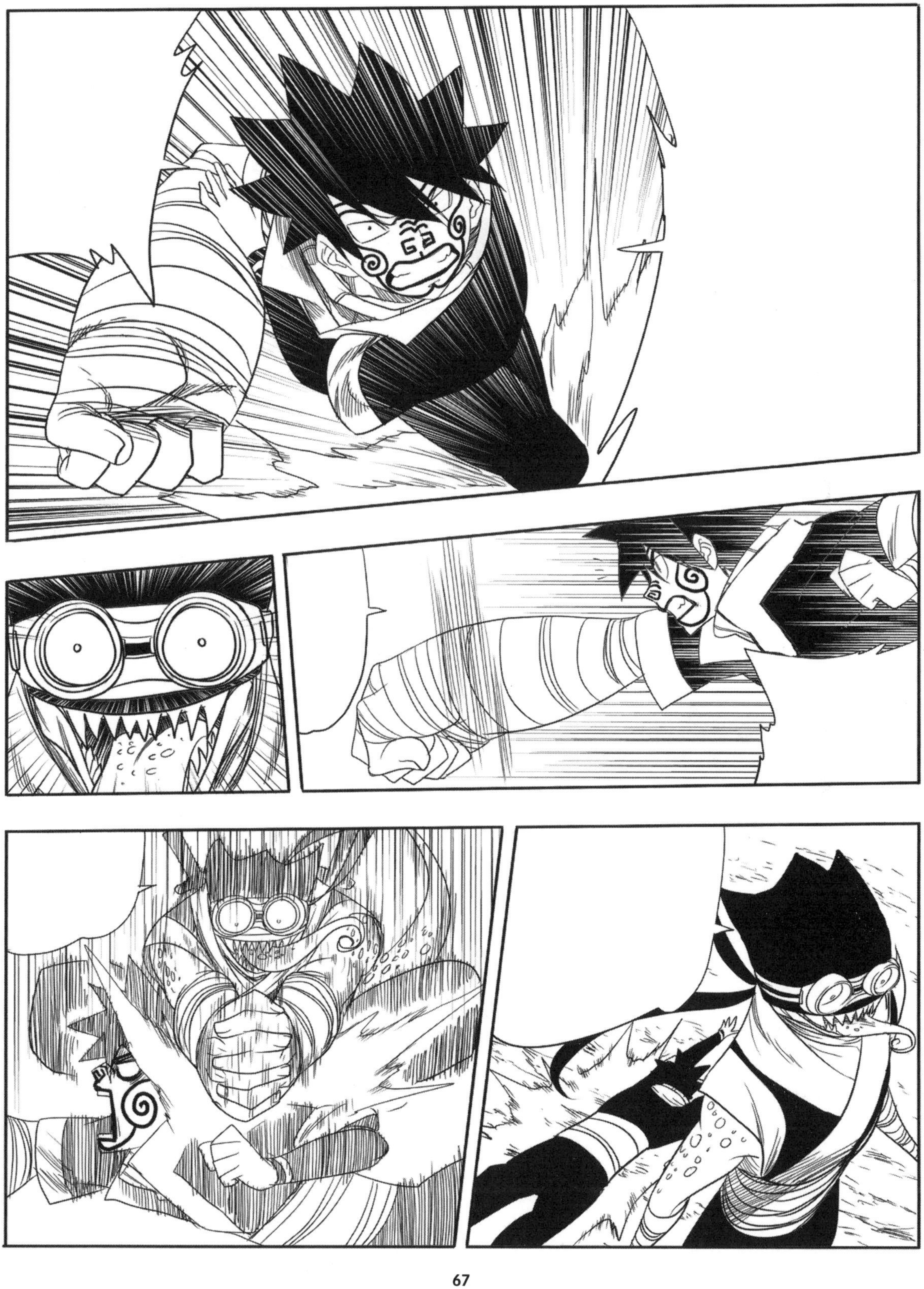

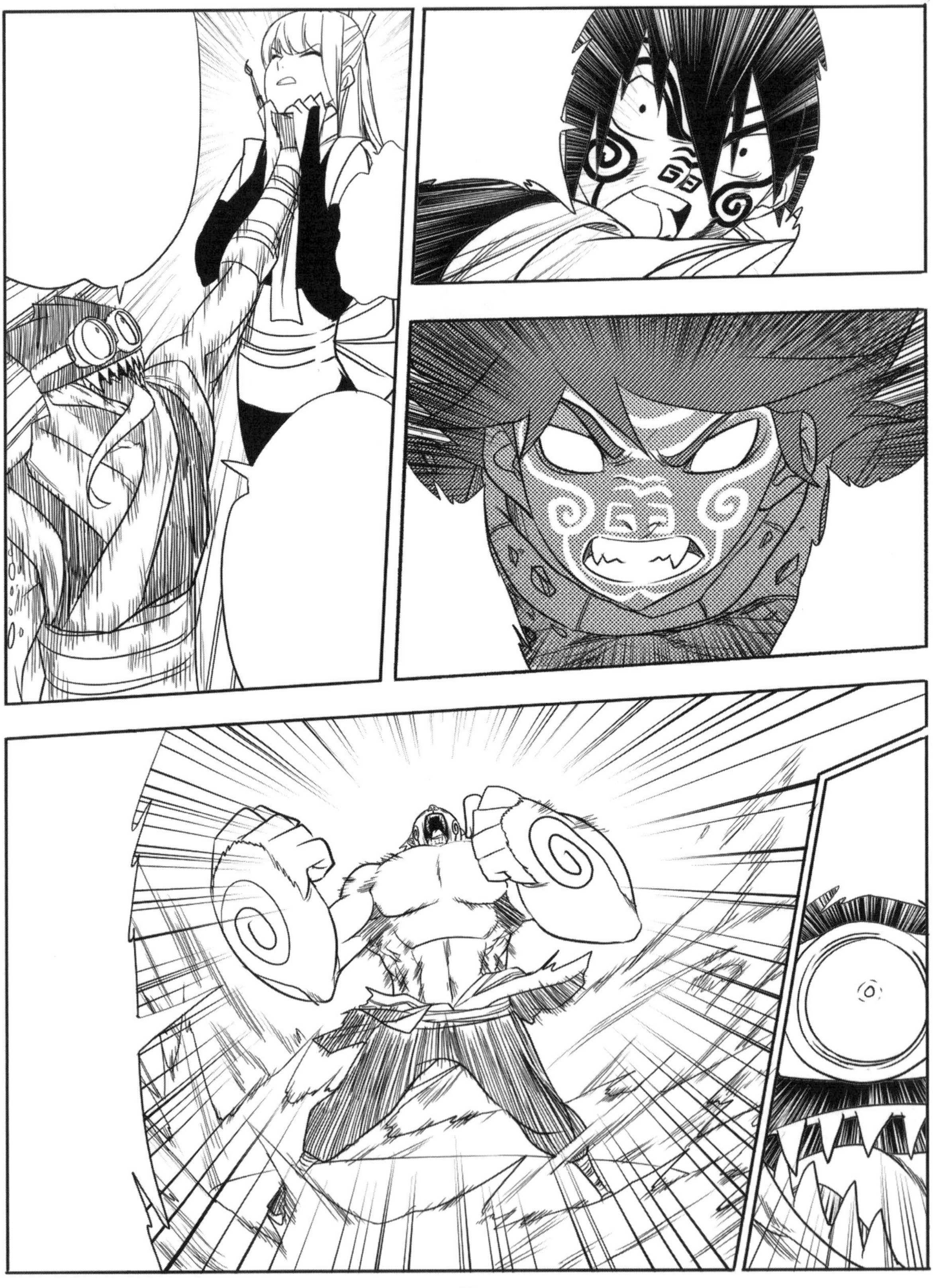

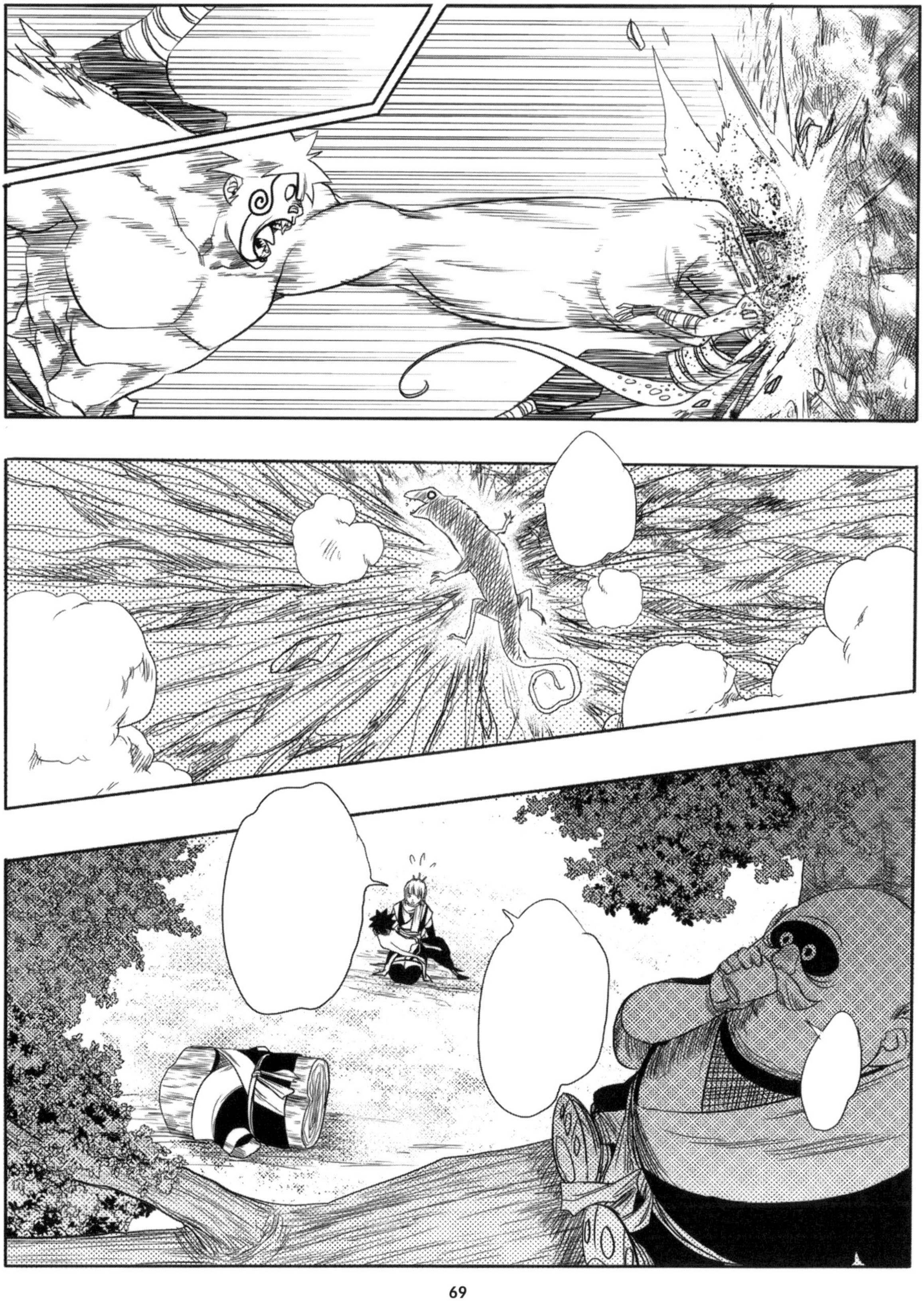

STORY #6

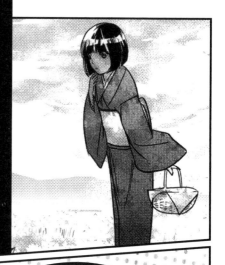

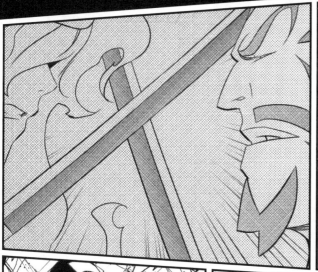

ARTIST:

ERWIN PRASETYA

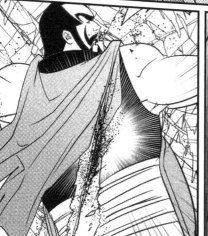

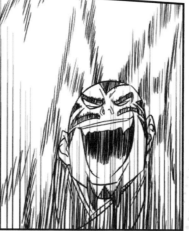

TITLE:

_____

_____

_____

WRITER:

_____

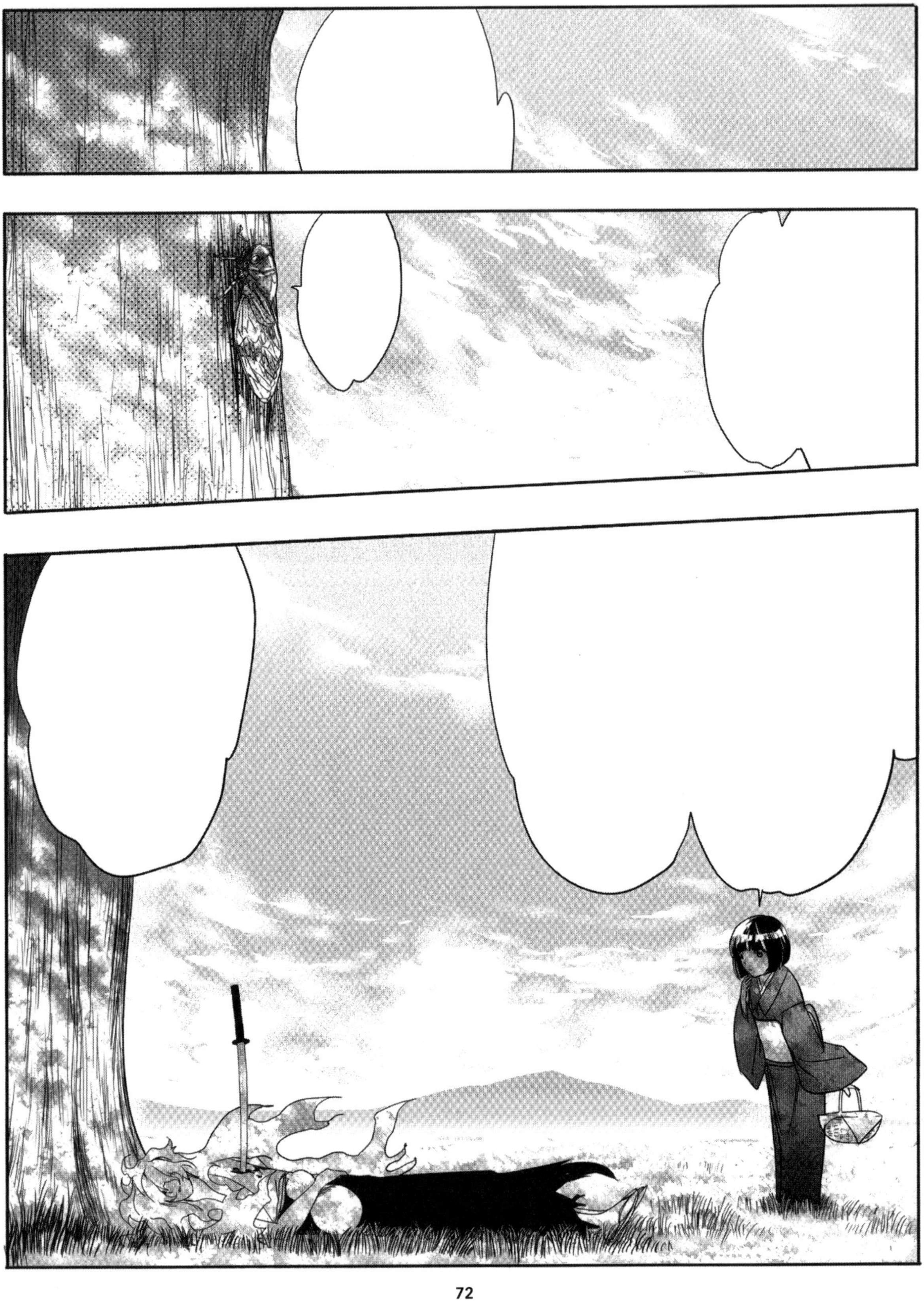

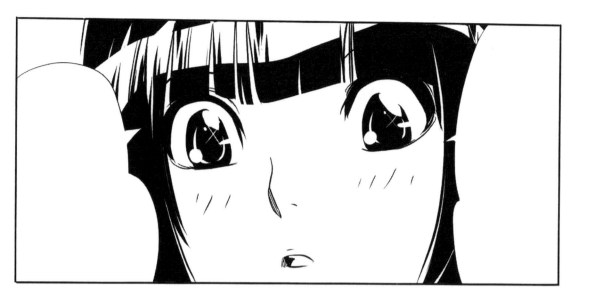

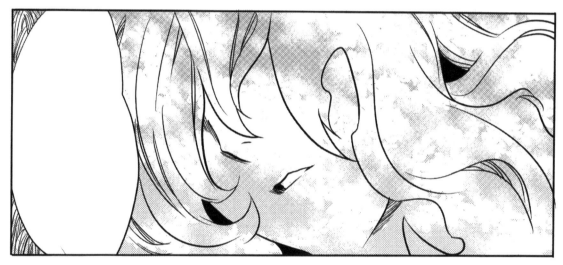

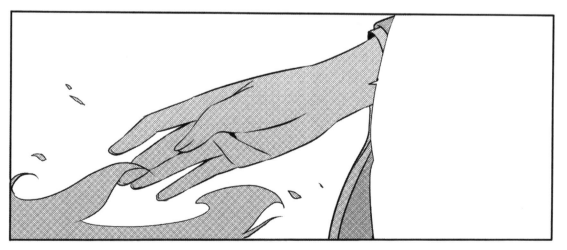

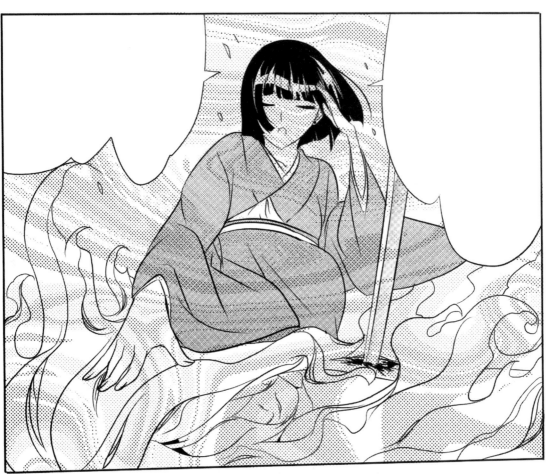

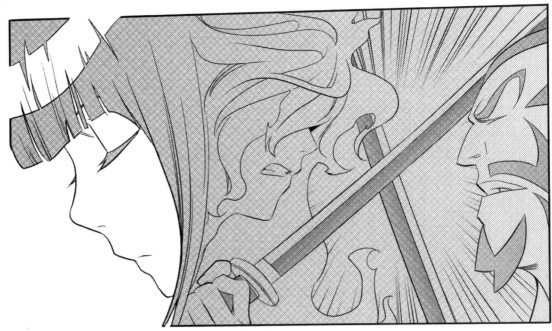

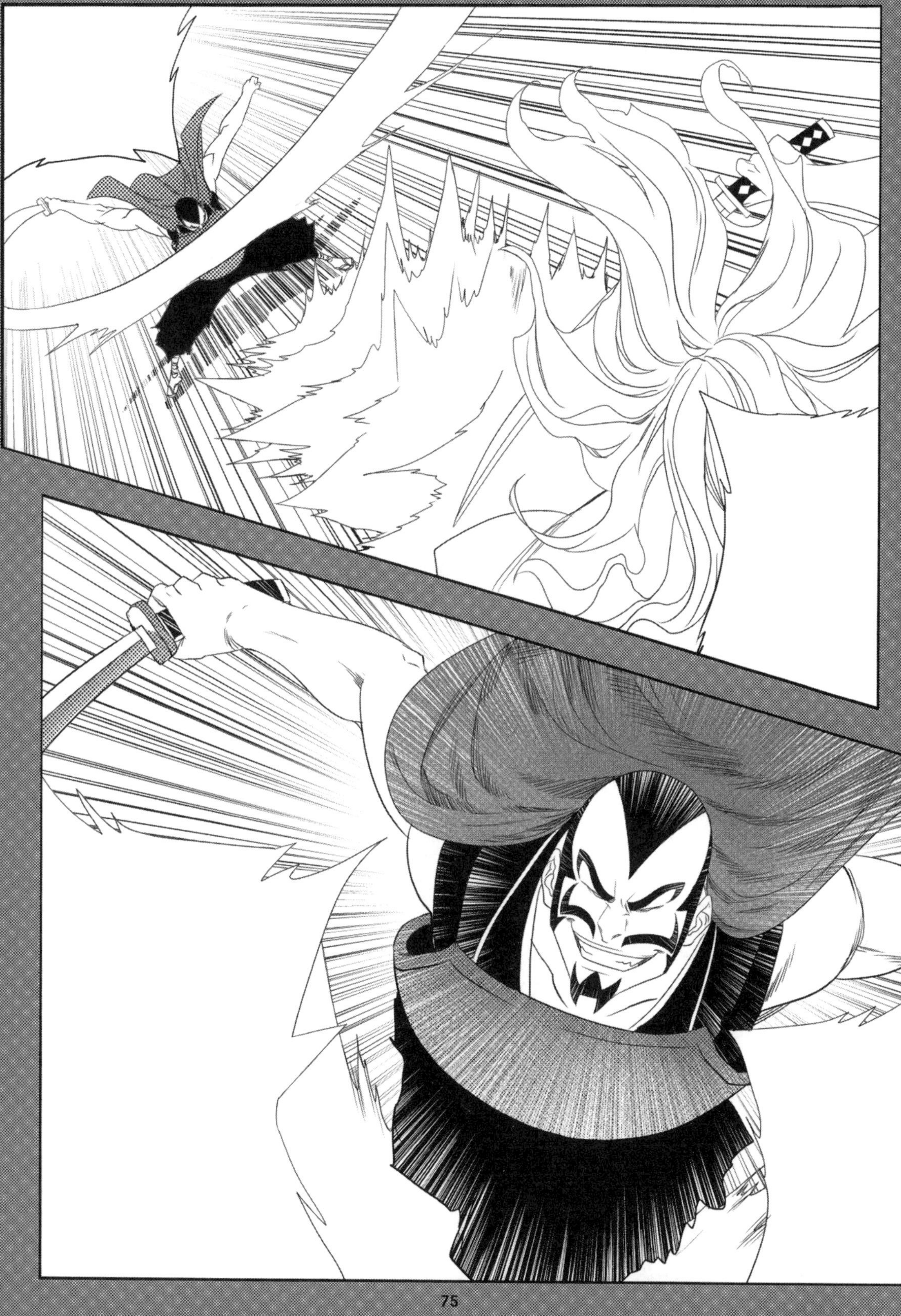

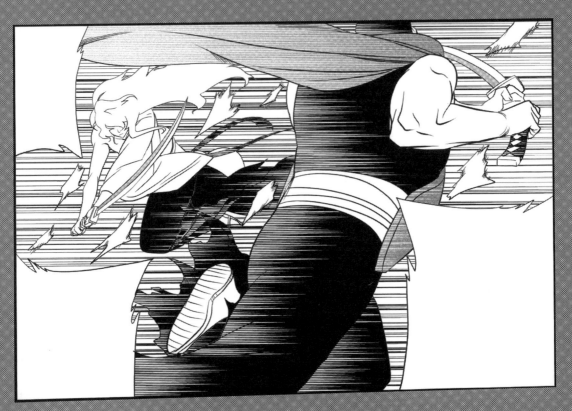

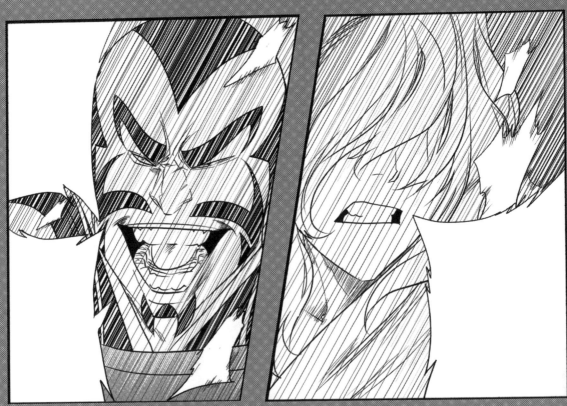

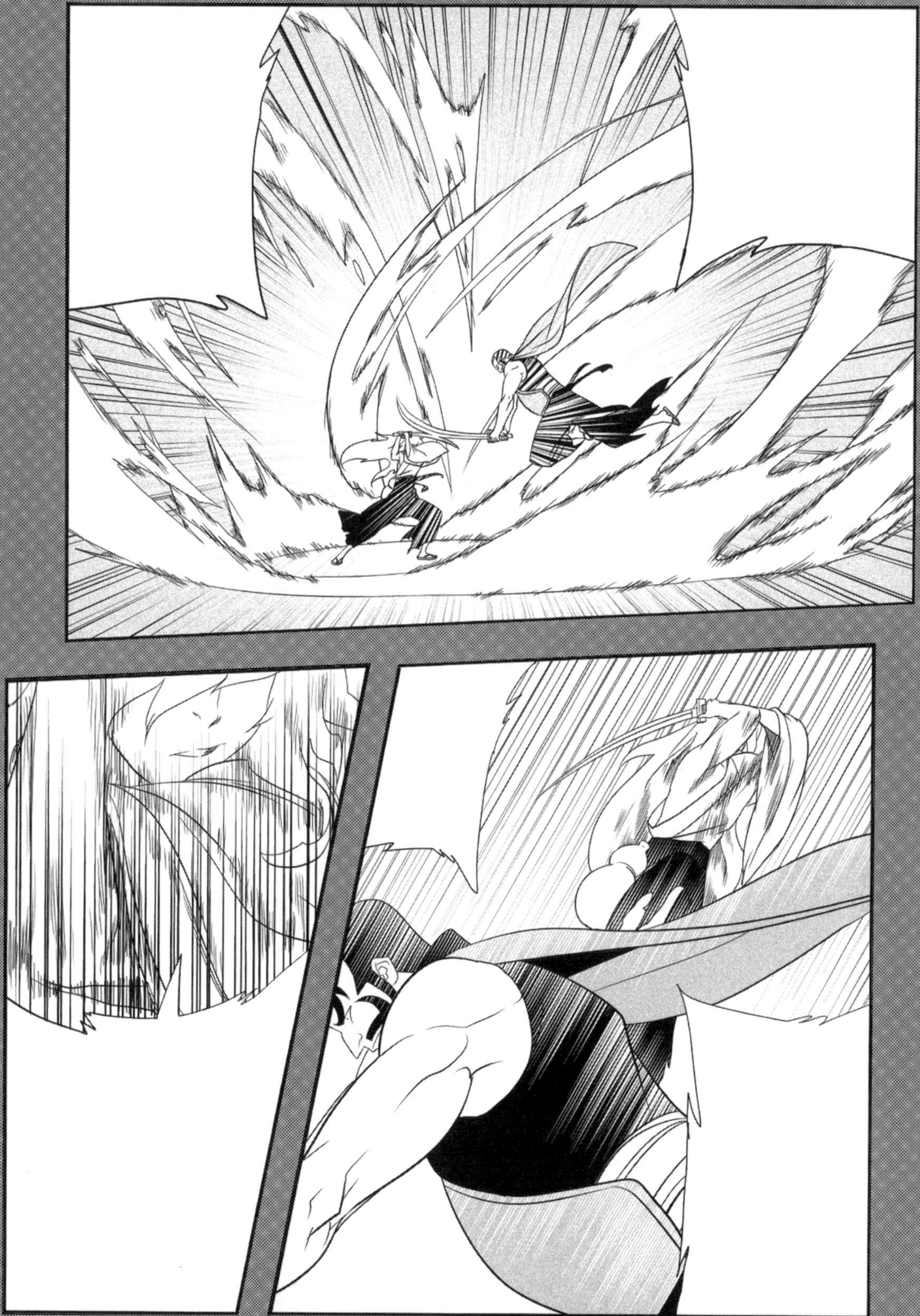

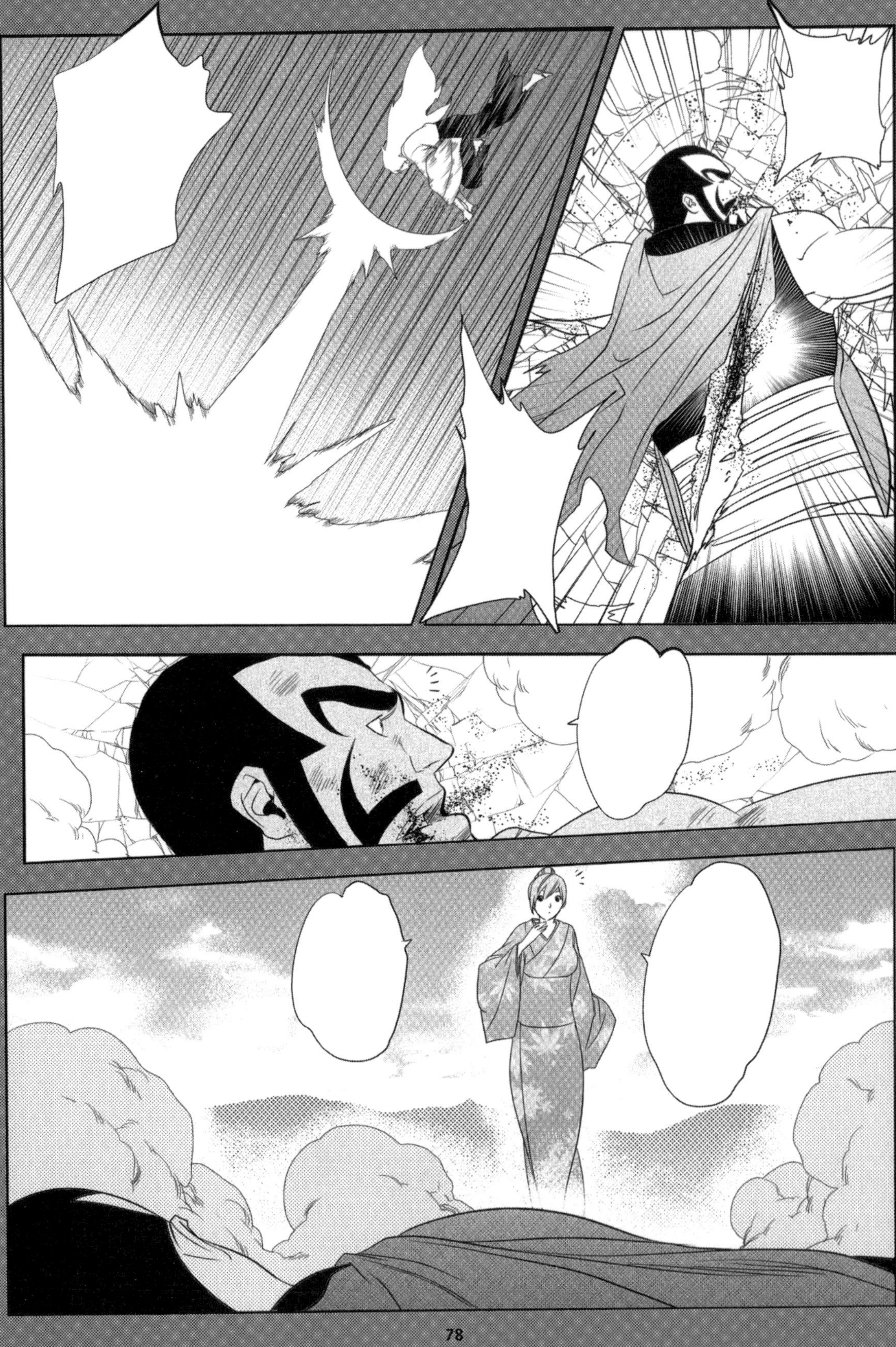

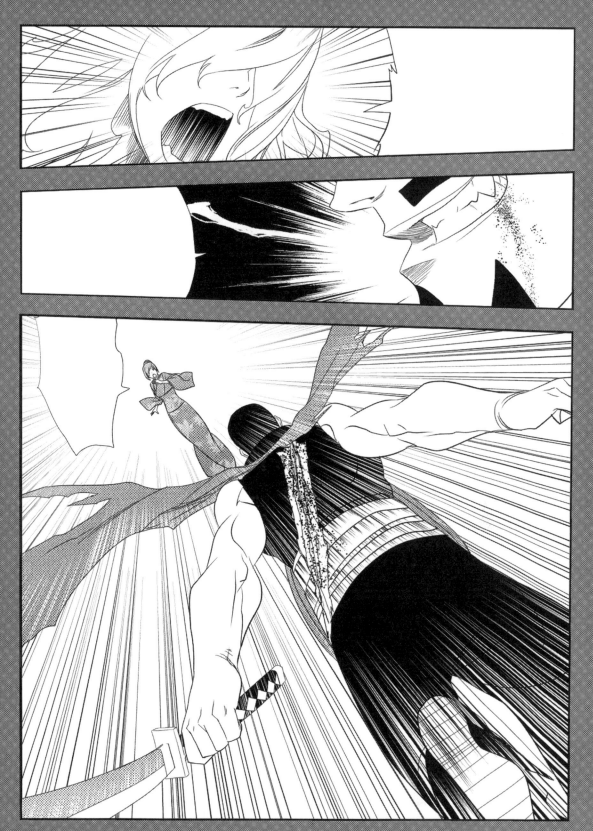

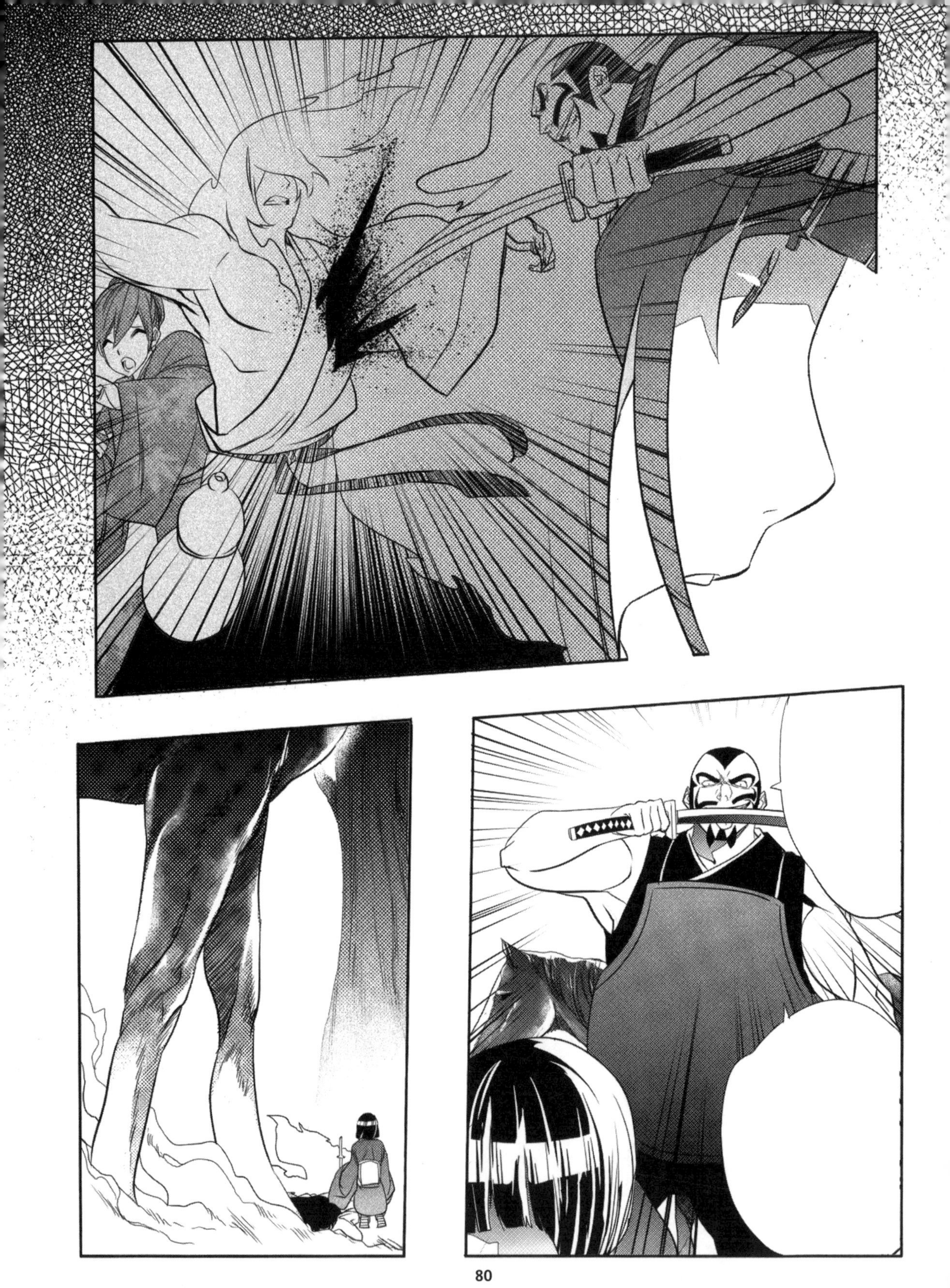

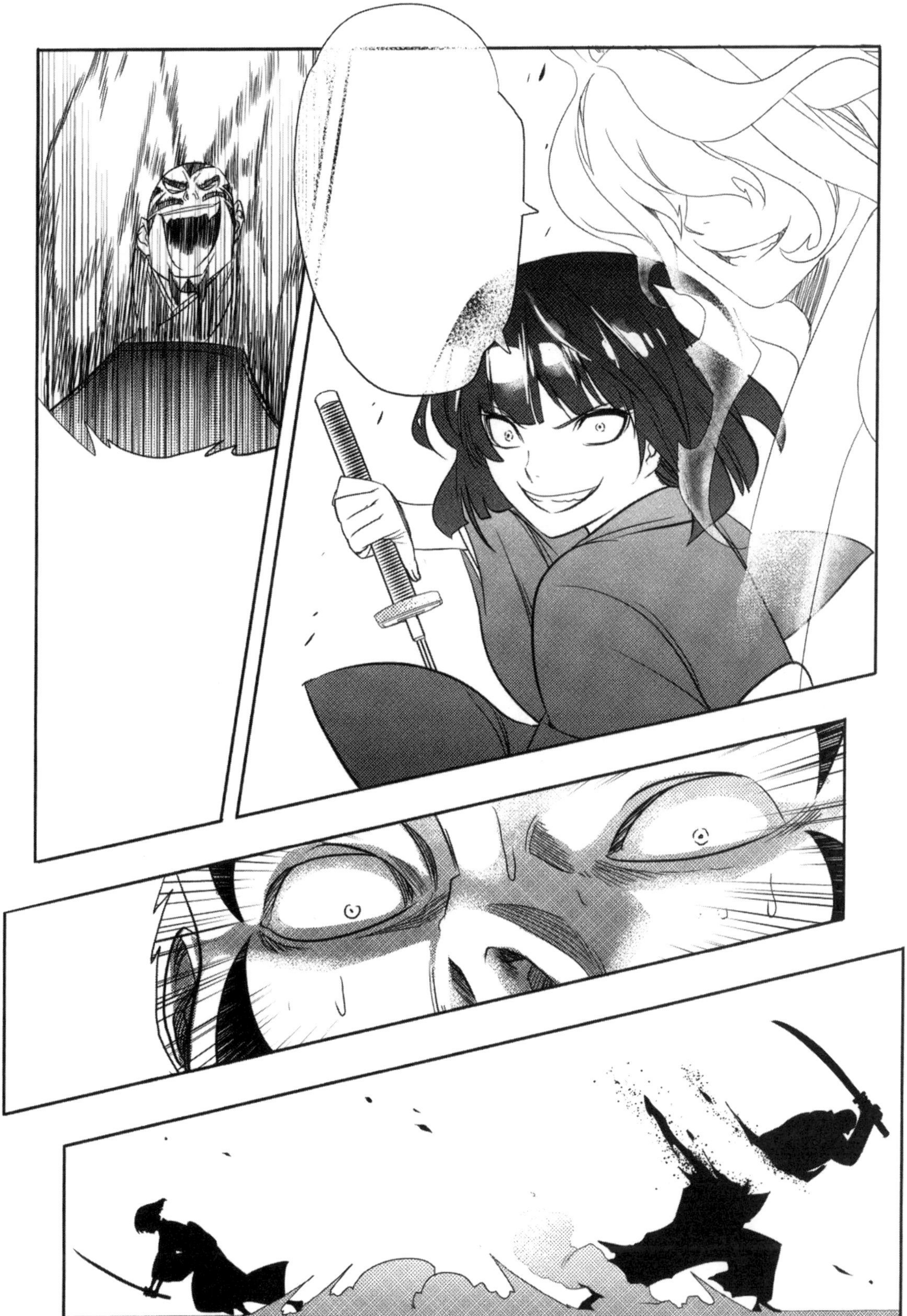

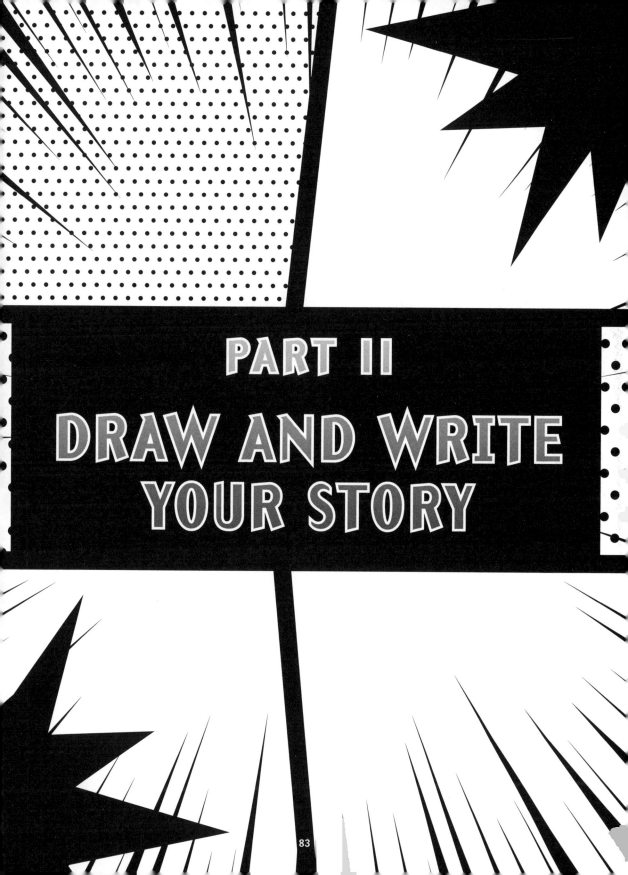

PART II
DRAW AND WRITE YOUR STORY

In this part of *Make Your Own Manga*, let your inner artist fly free! In the blank panels provided, draw the characters and action you'd like to take place in your story (or stories) and then supply the words and sounds you'd like to accompany them. Don't worry about making your drawings look professional; the point is for you to have fun and use your imagination. If you create multiple stories, don't forget to use the Contents page to give each story a title and starting page number. That way, you'll be able to easily find each of your manga and update them whenever inspiration strikes. There are two two-panel spreads, one at the beginning and one at the end, so you can begin and end your works with a bang! Get ready, get set, draw!

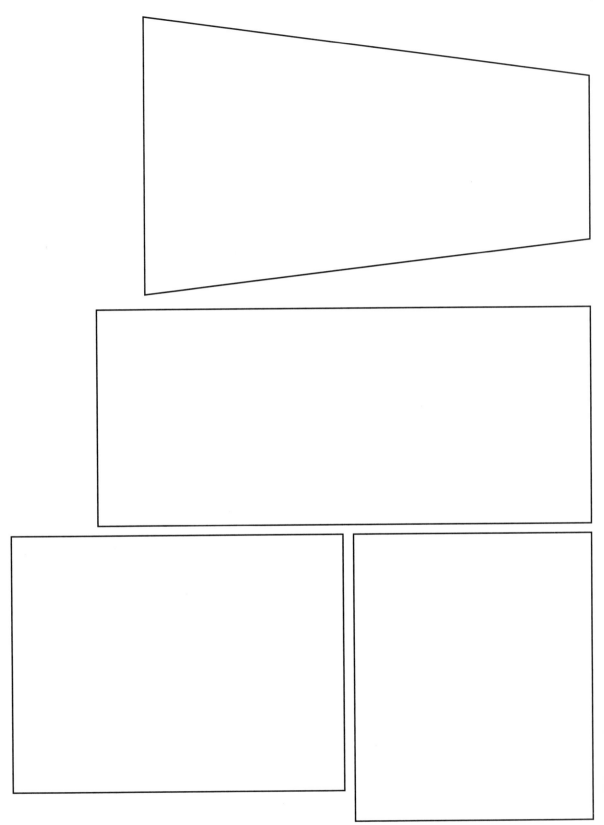

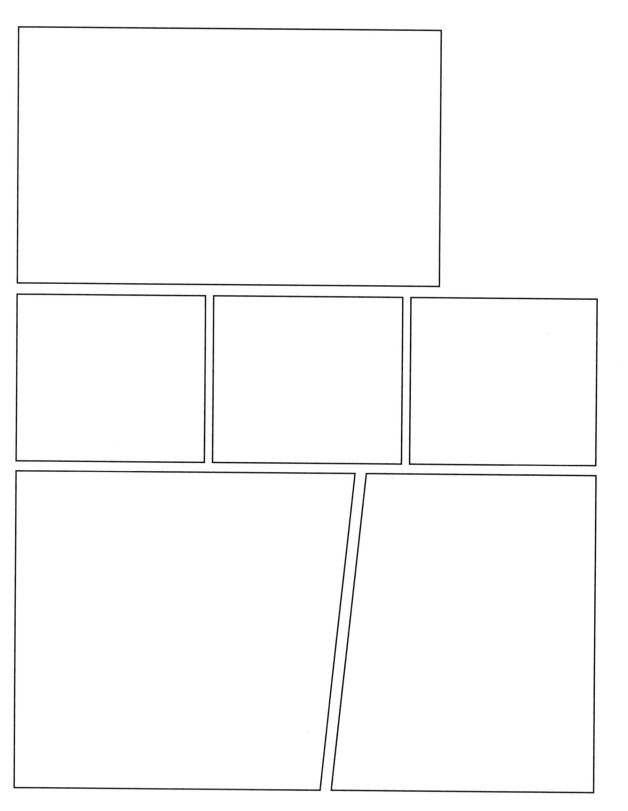

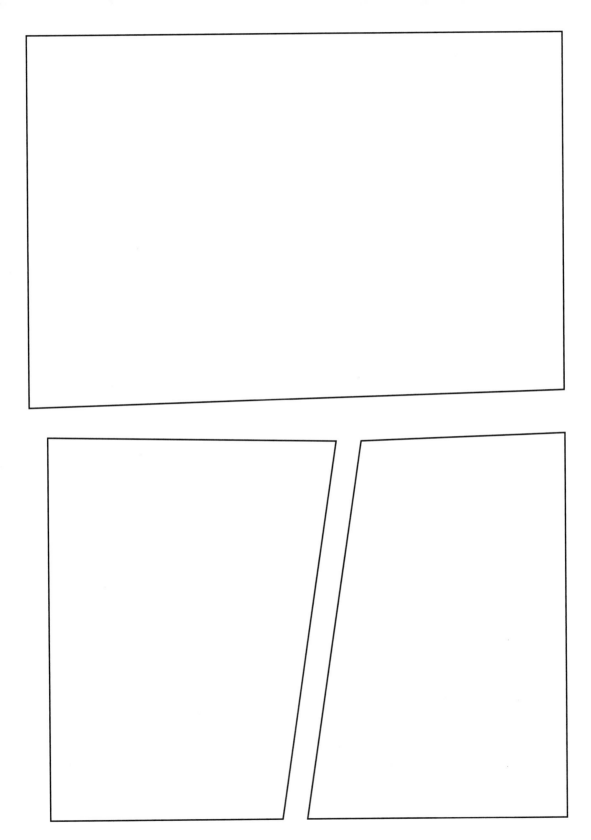

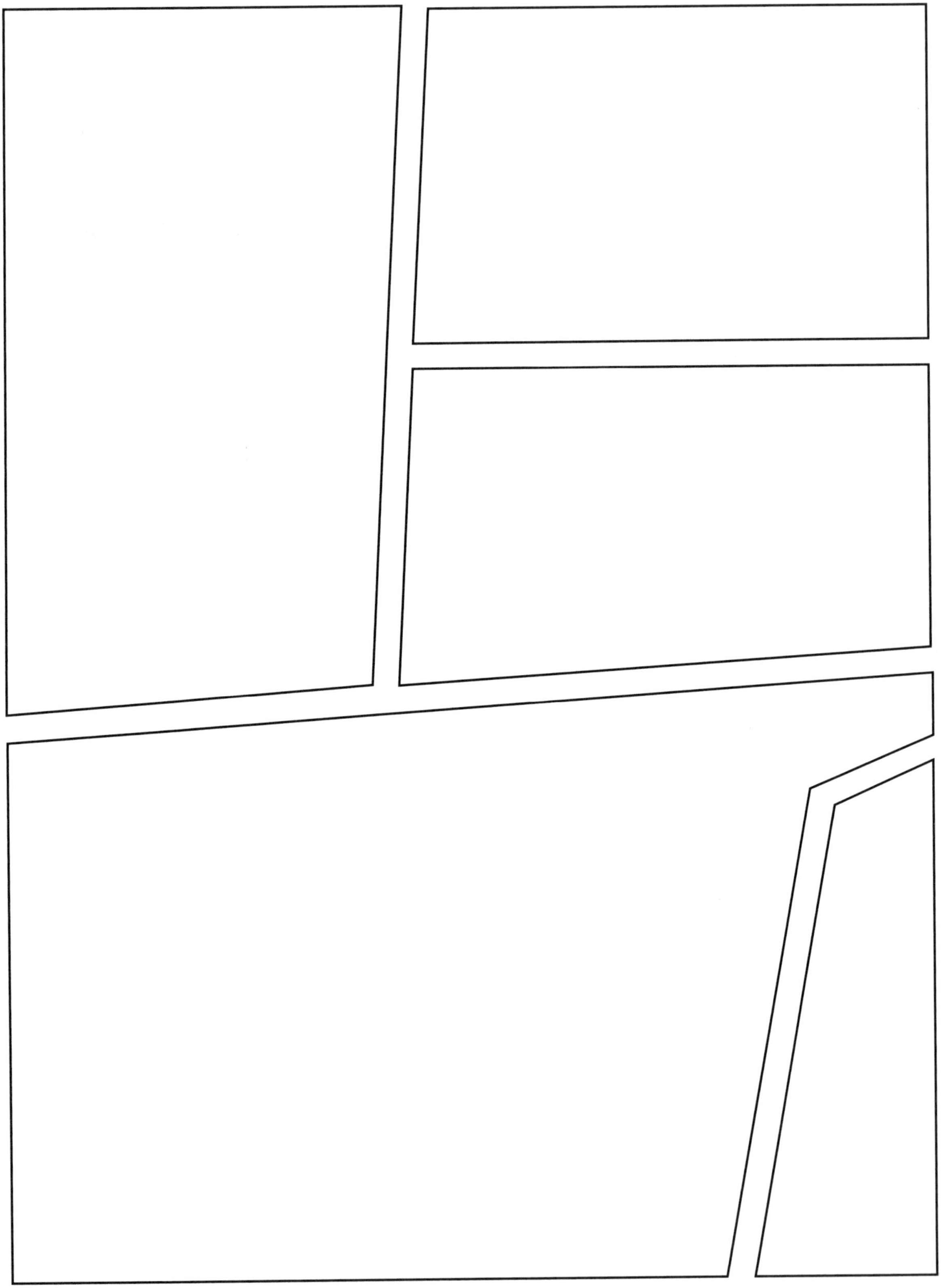

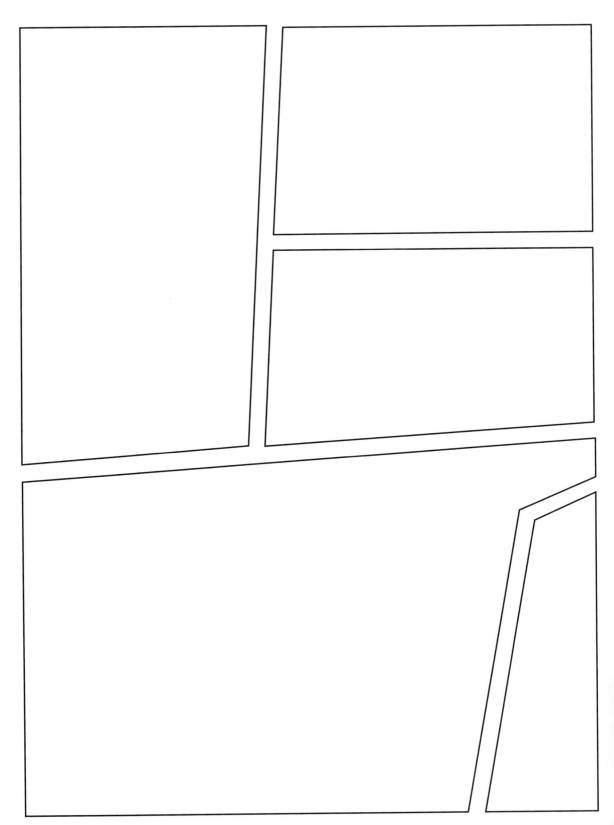

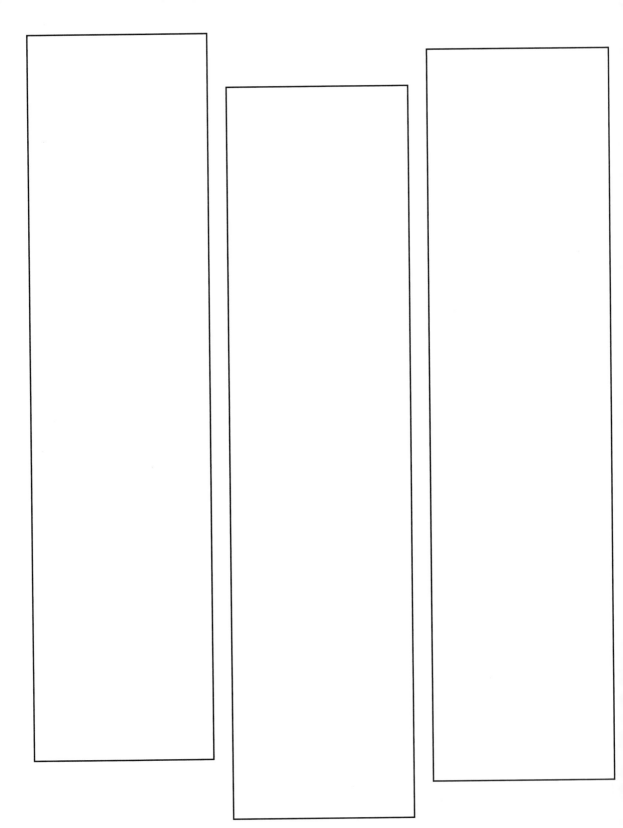

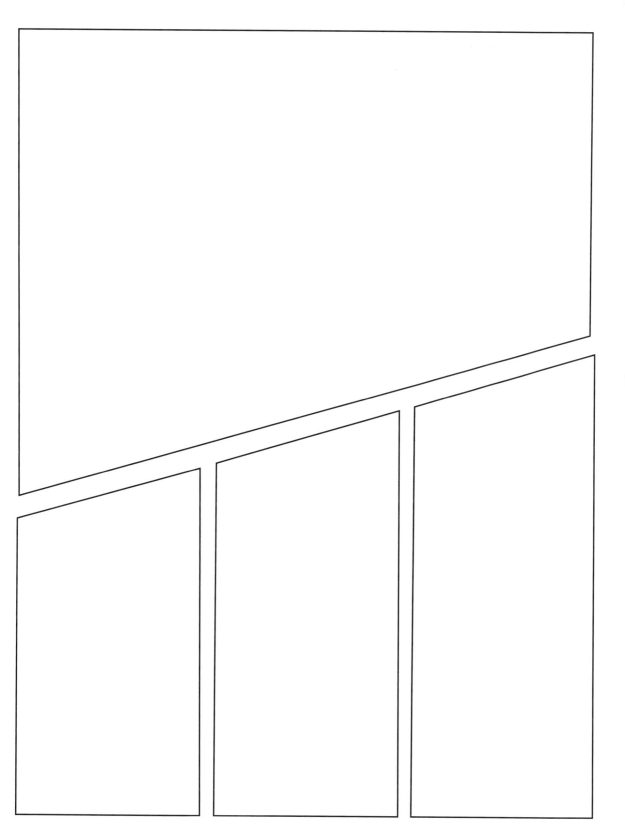

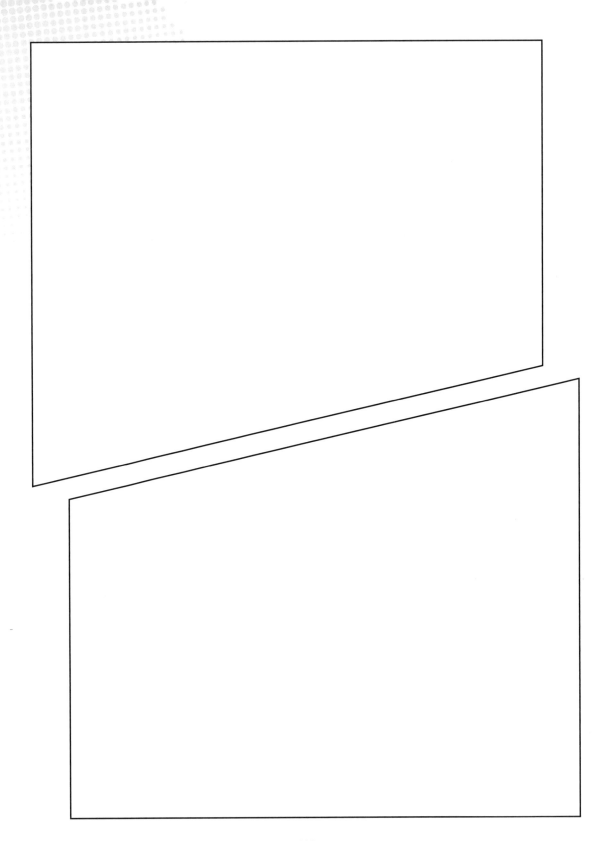

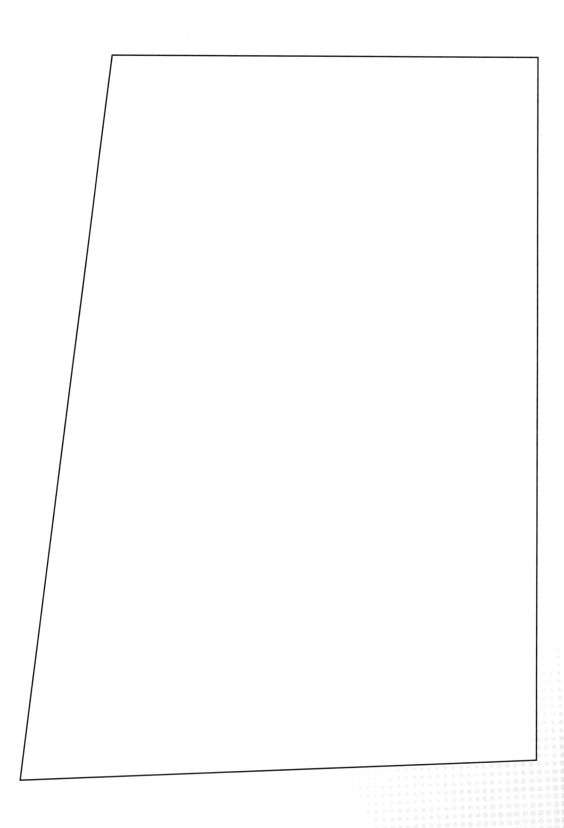

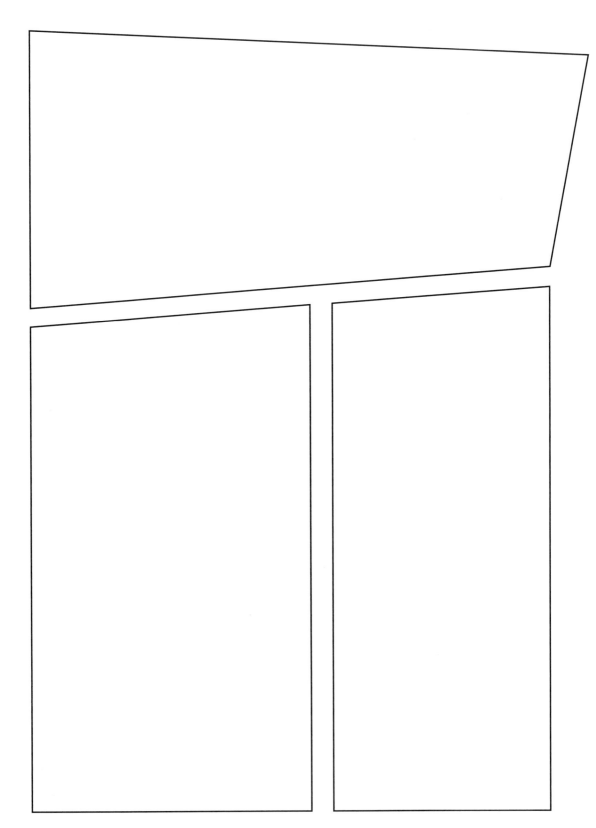

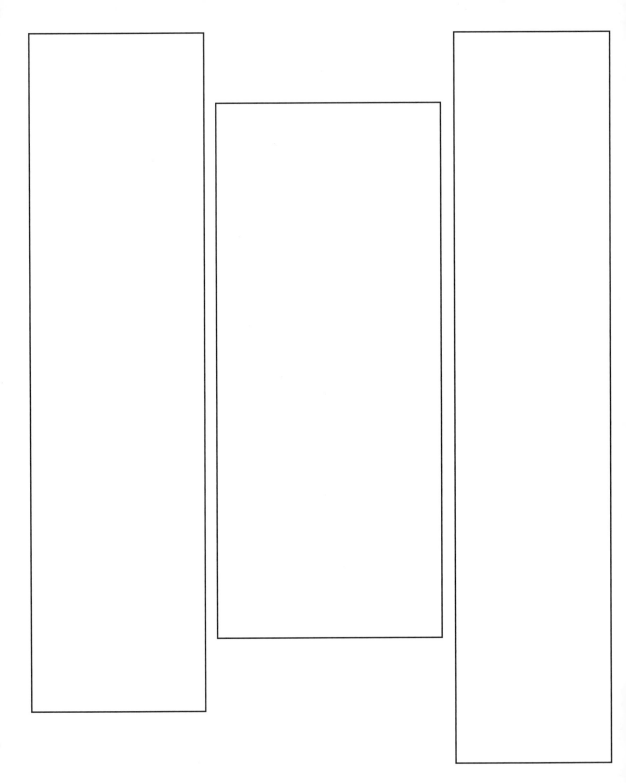

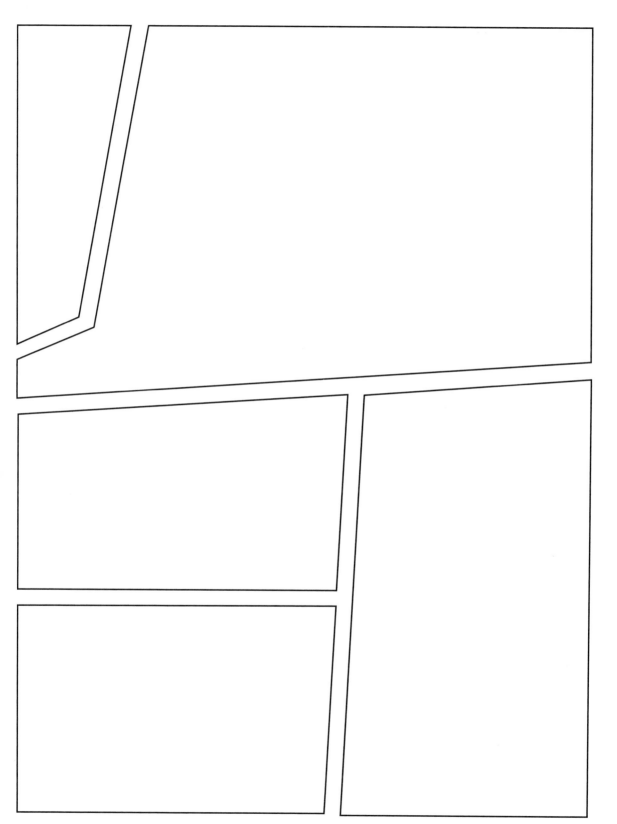

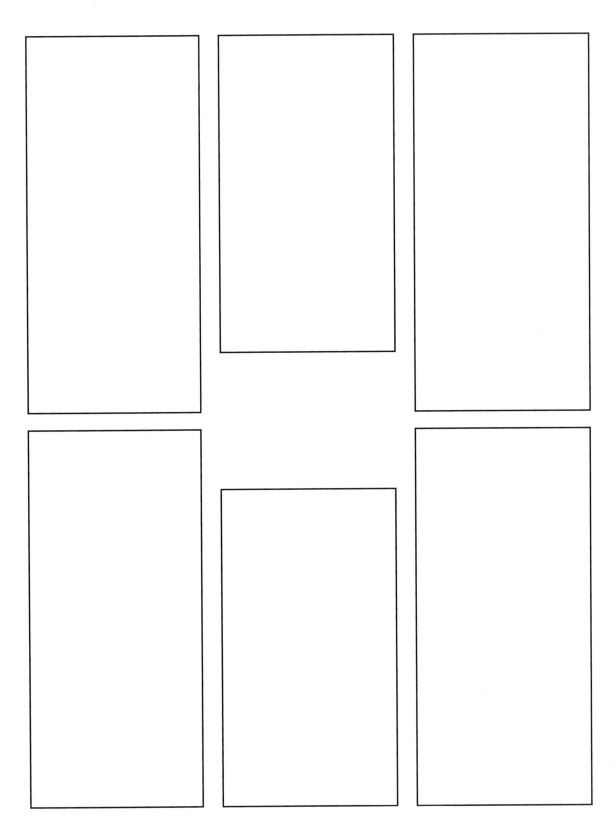

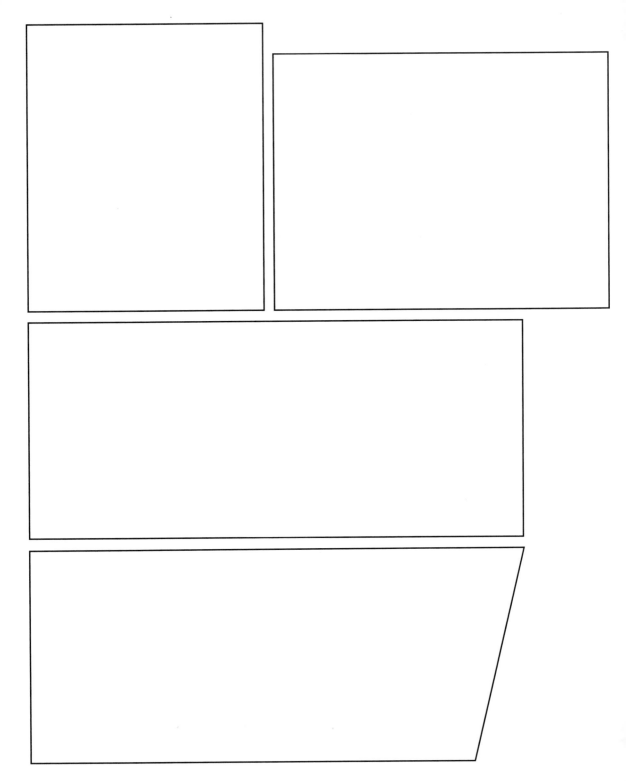

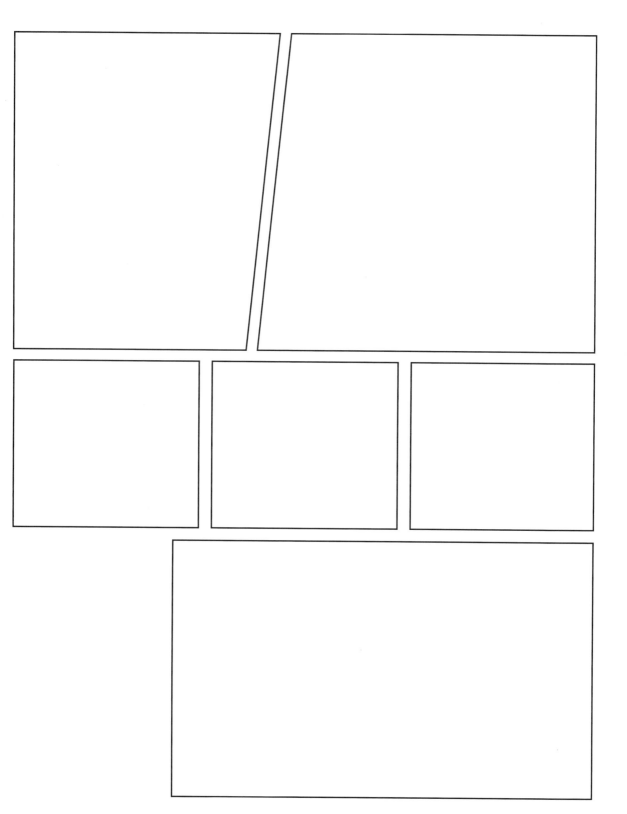

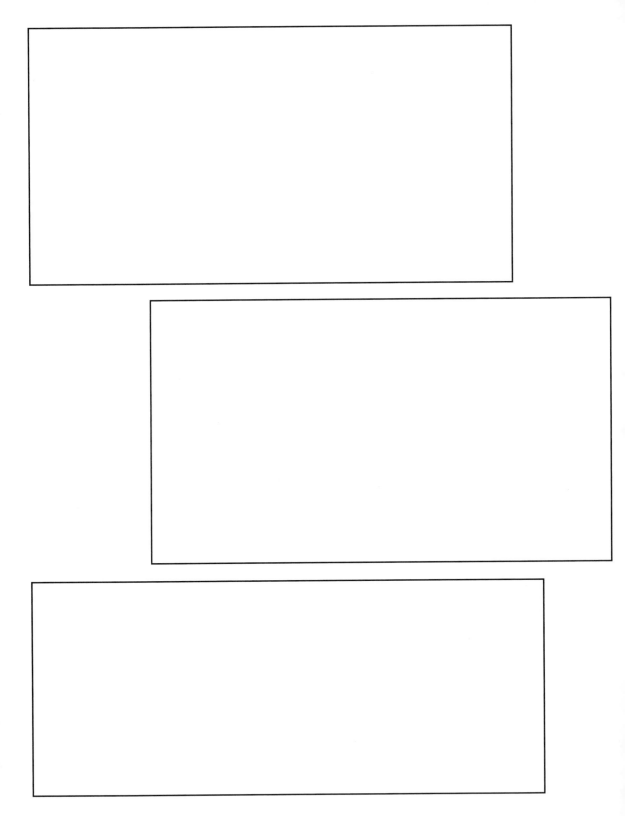

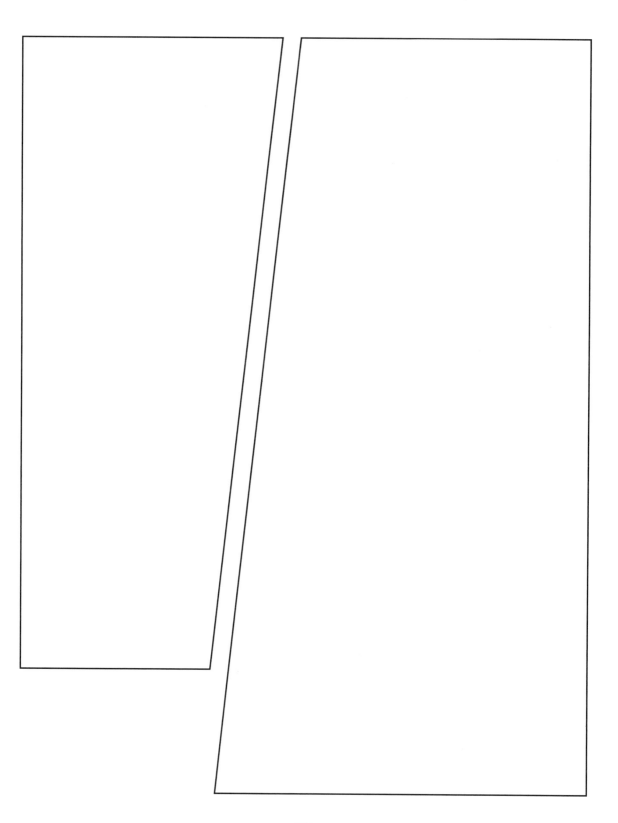

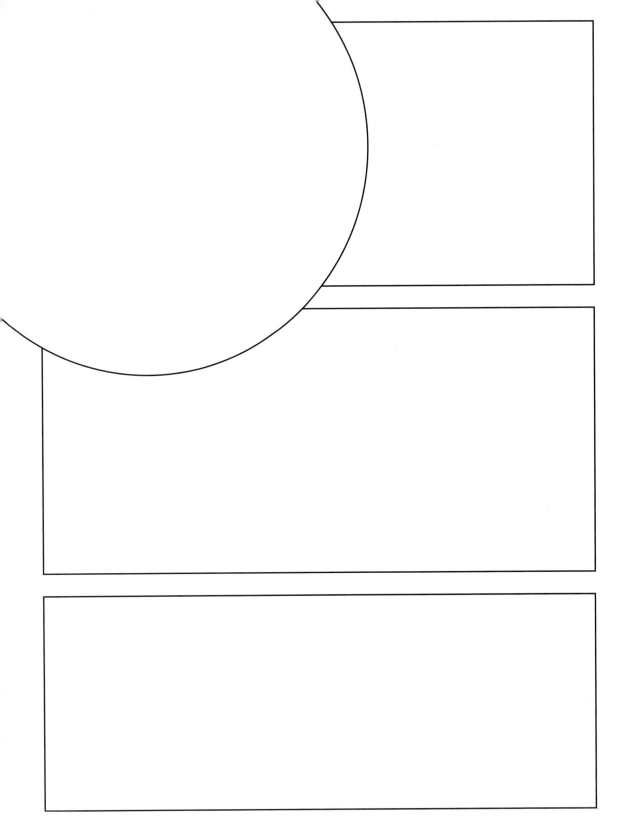

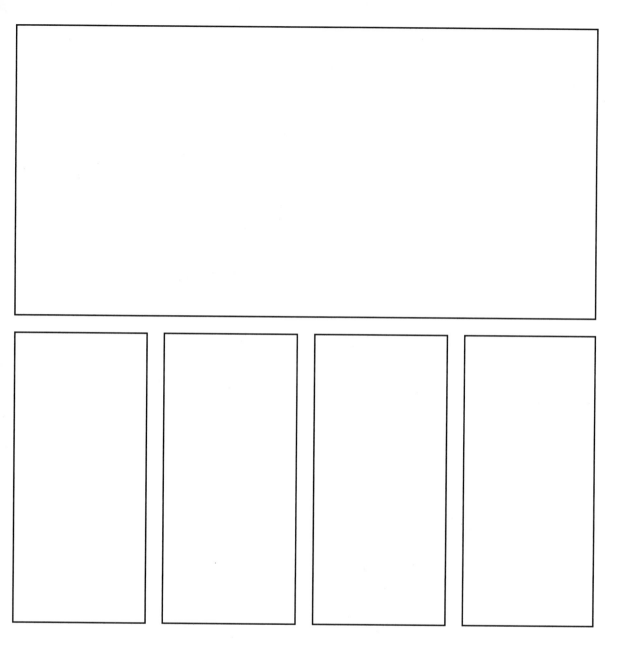

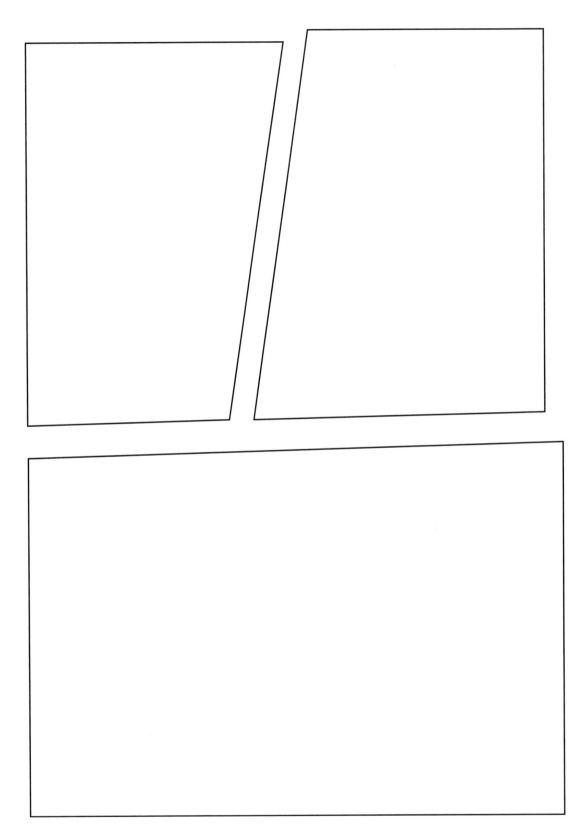

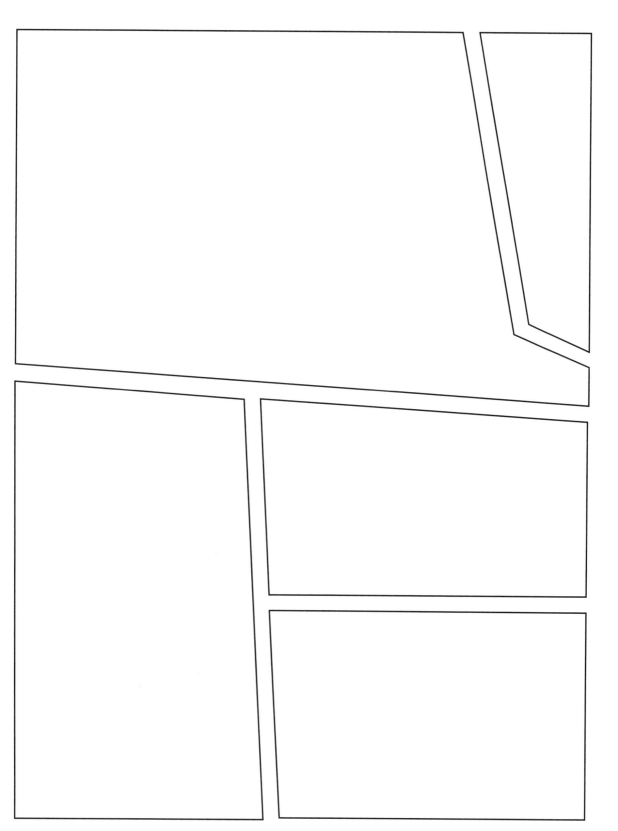

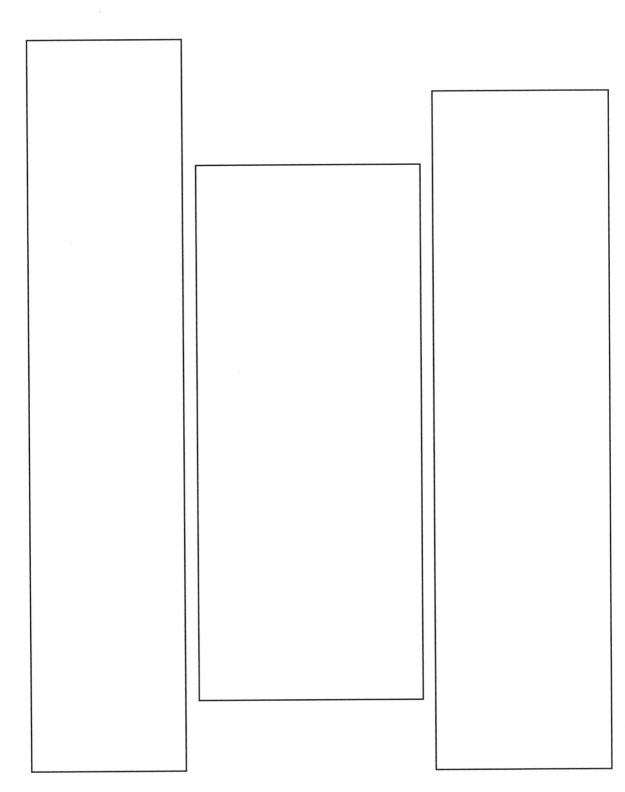

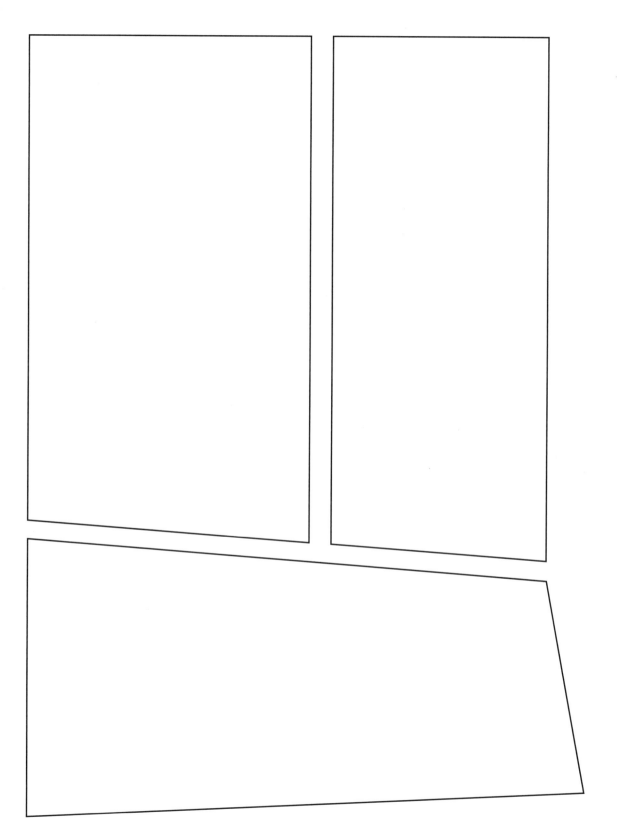

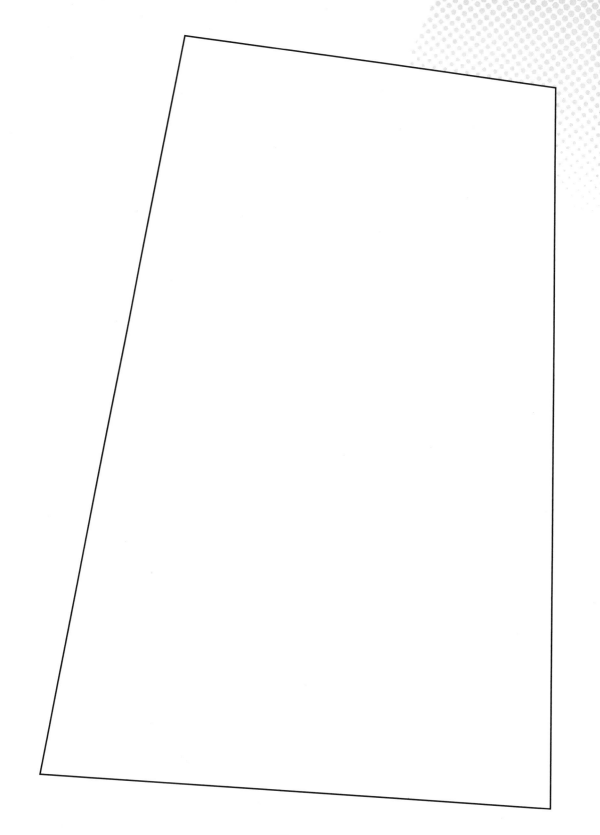

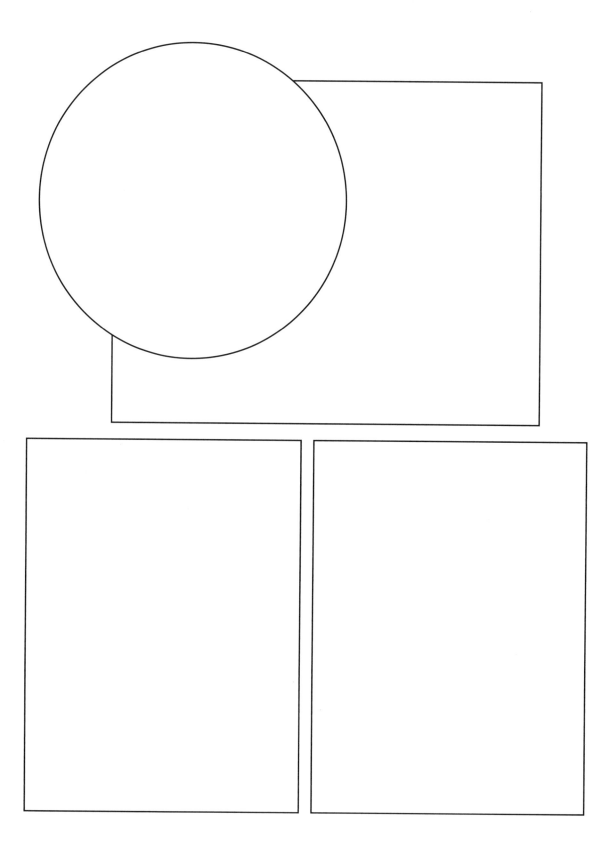

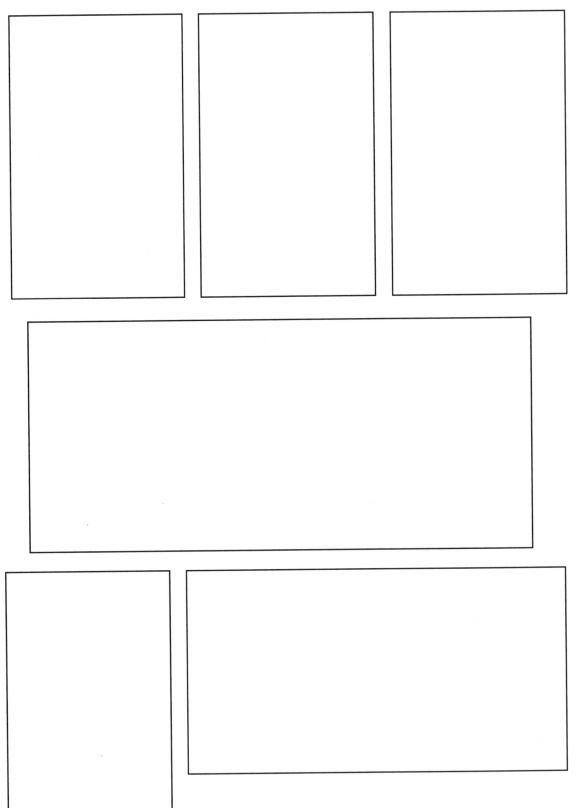

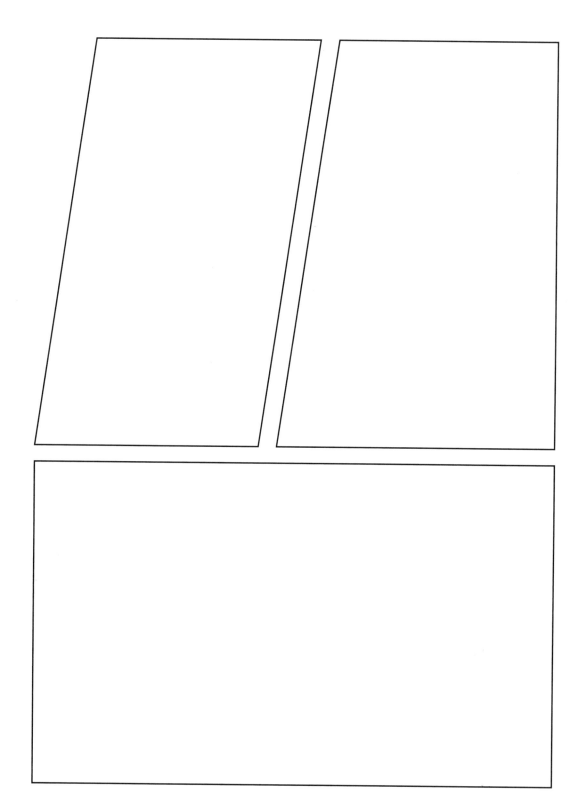

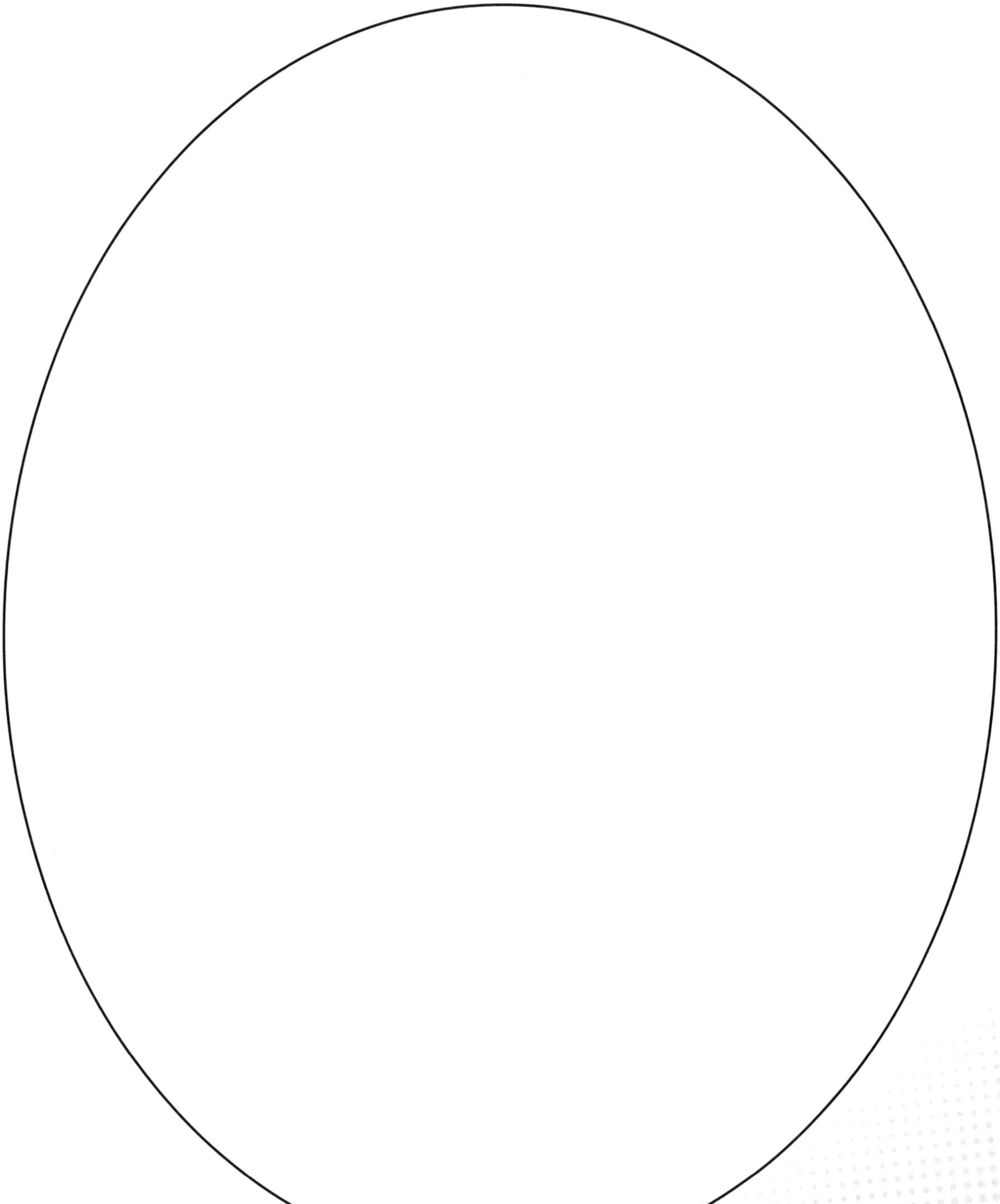

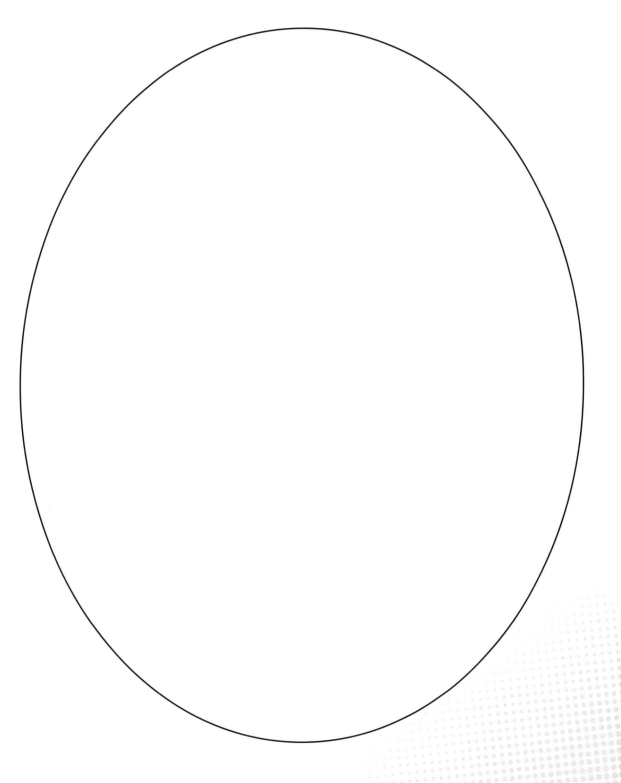

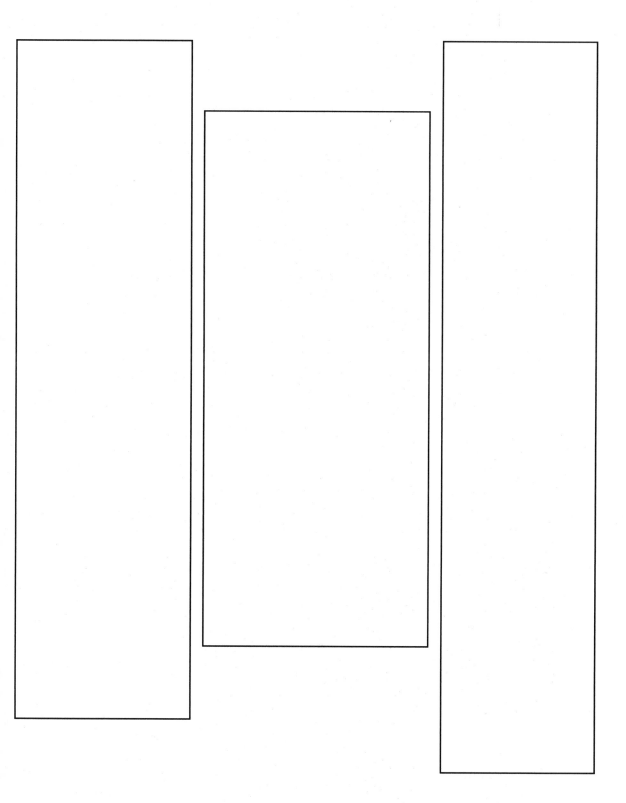

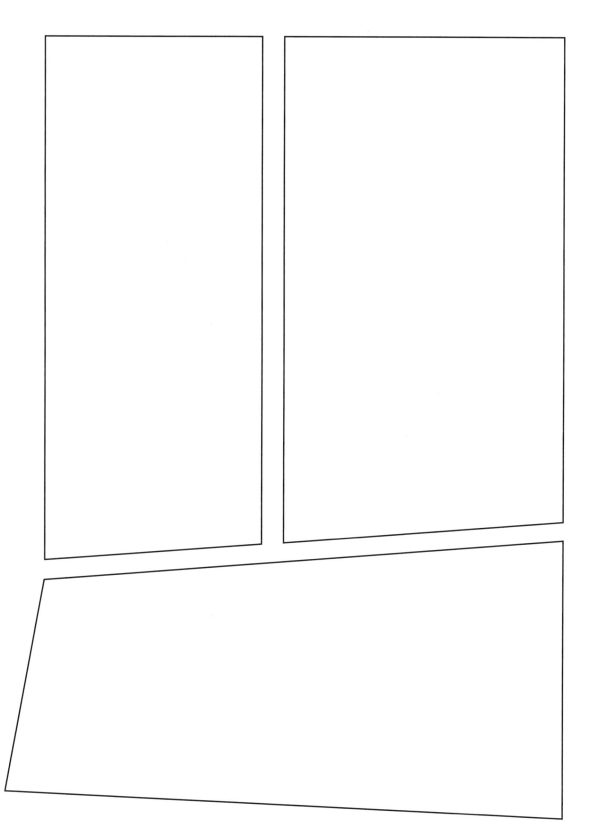

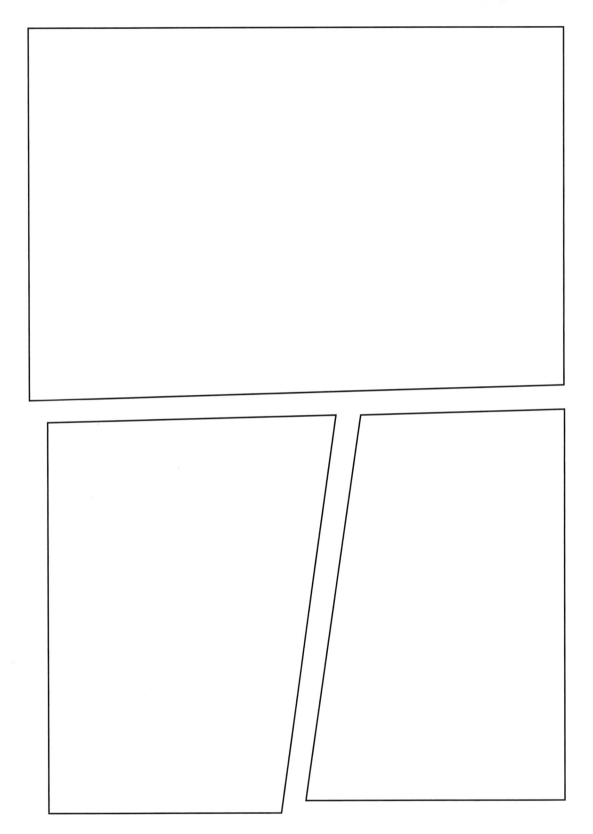

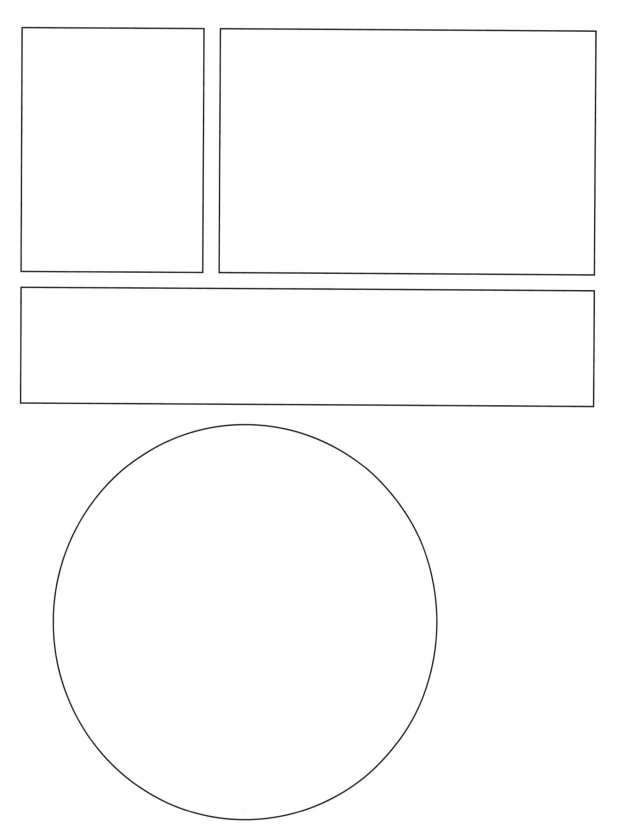

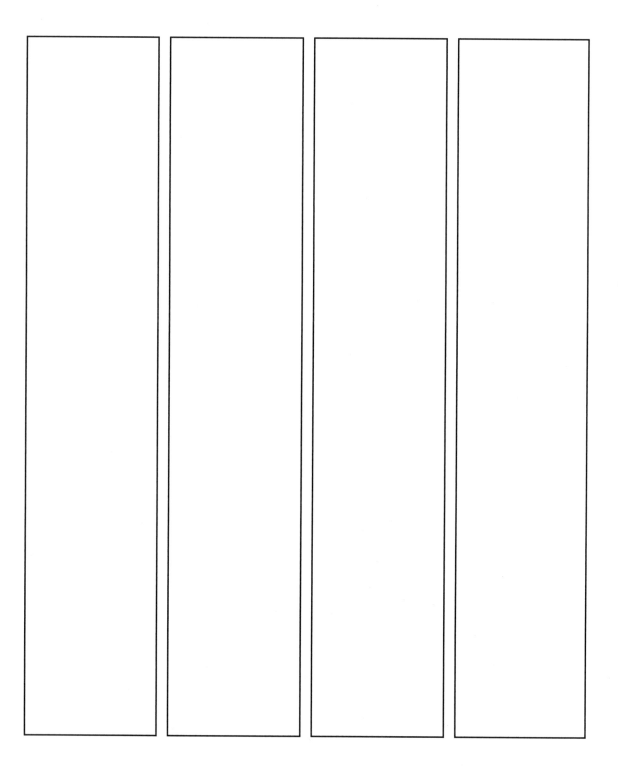

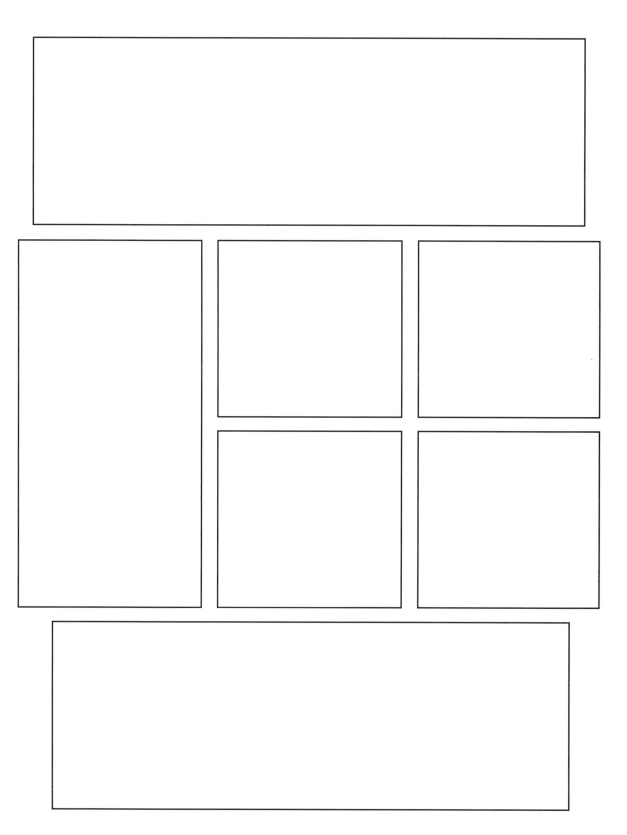

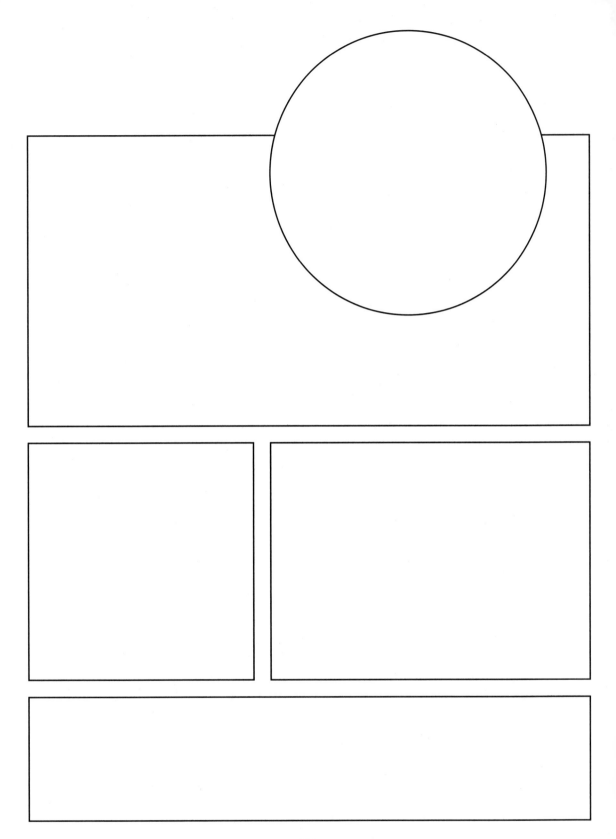

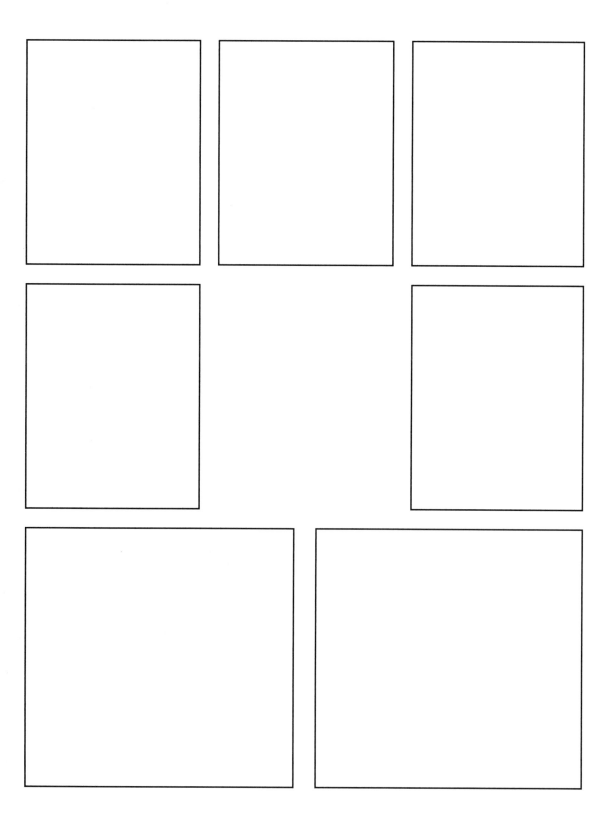

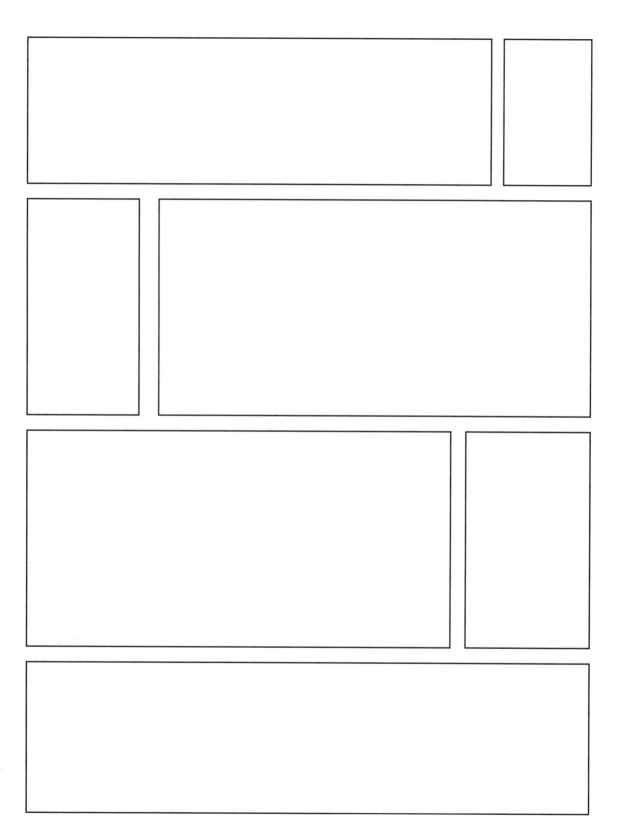

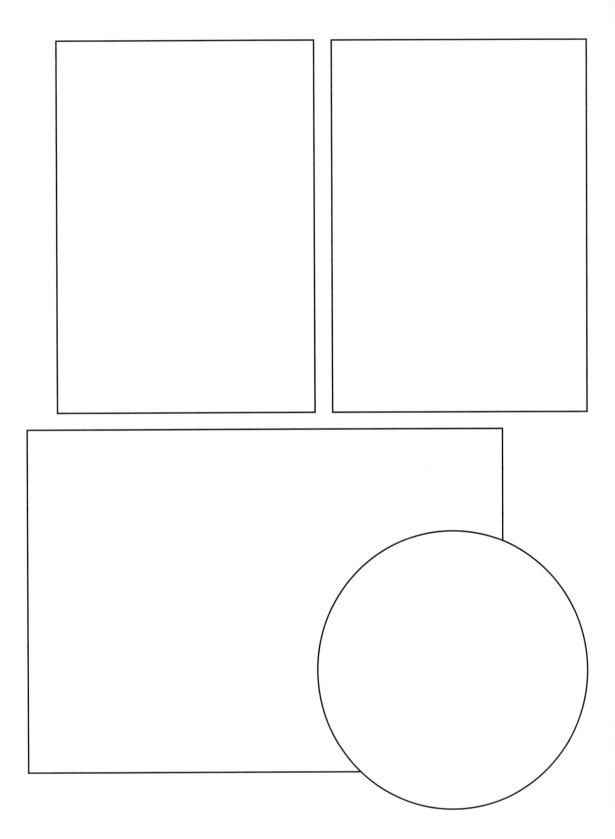

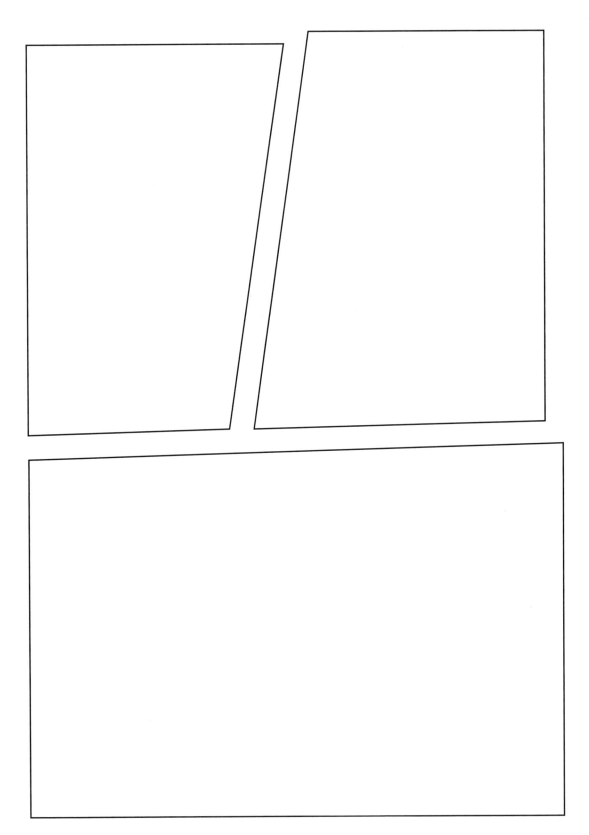

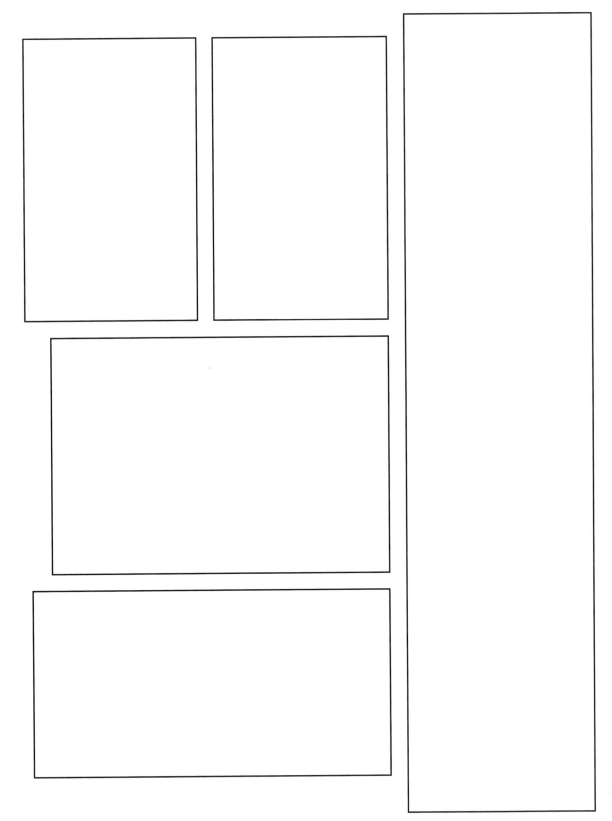

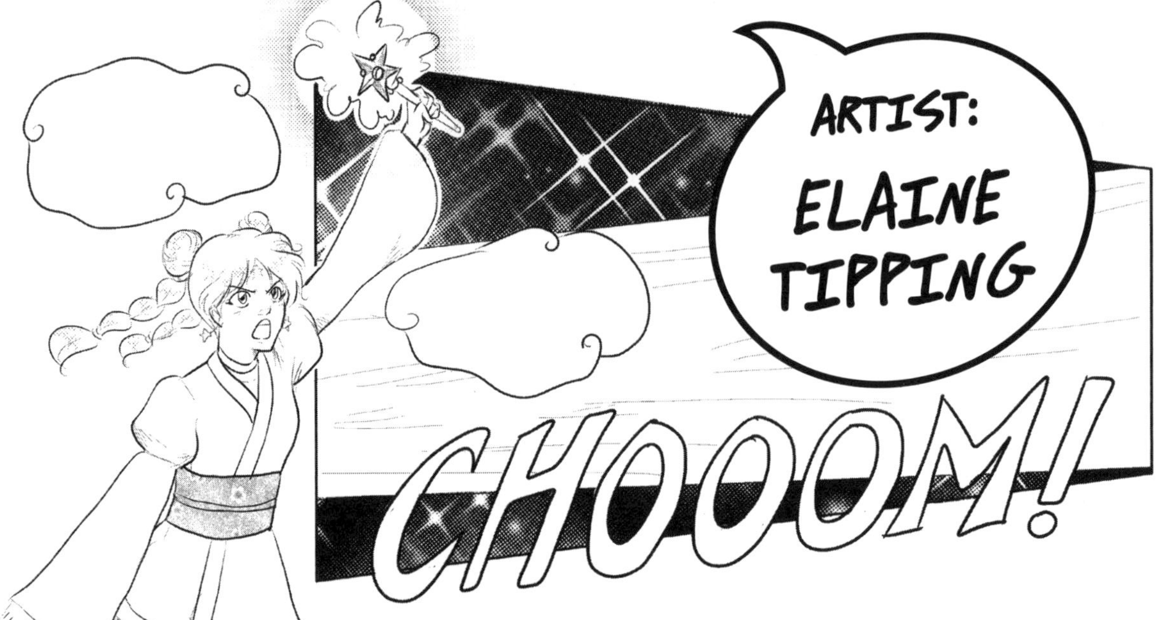
ARTIST:
ELAINE TIPPING
CHOOOM!

ARTIST FOR STORIES #1, #3, AND #4

Elaine Tipping illustrates *Dubious Company*, *Licensed Heroes*, and a retelling of *Peter Pan* in manga format.

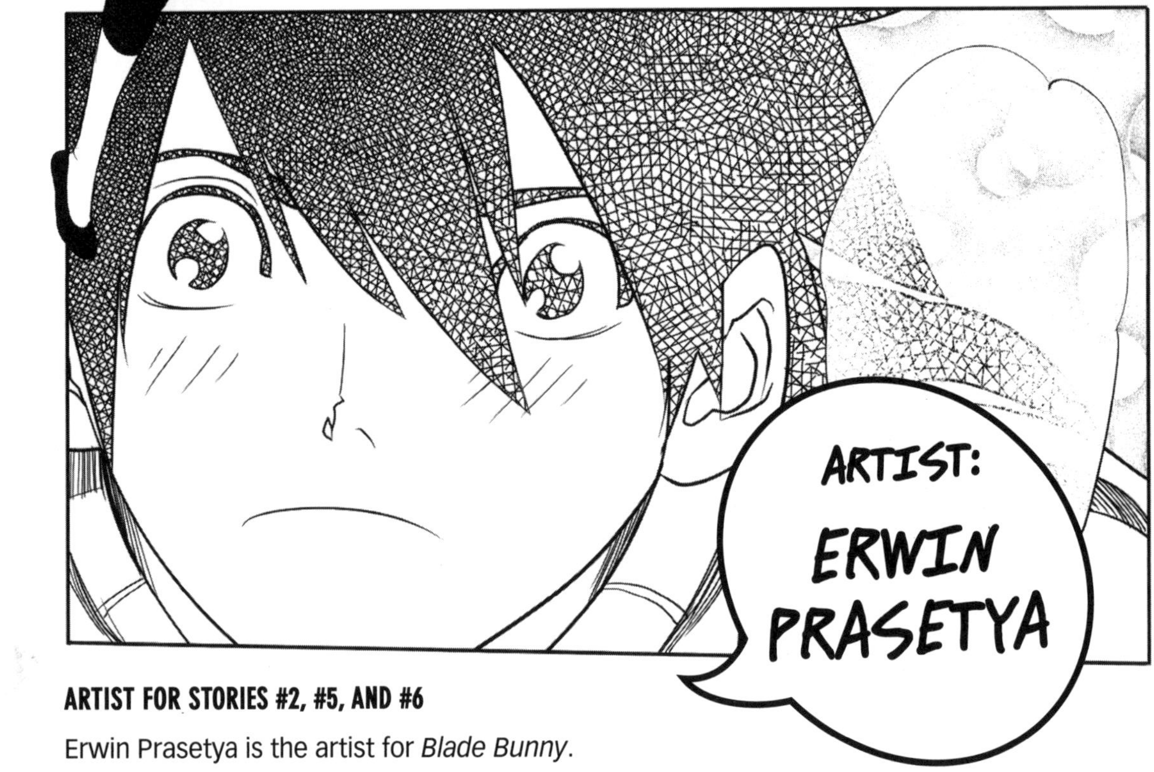
ARTIST:
ERWIN PRASETYA

ARTIST FOR STORIES #2, #5, AND #6

Erwin Prasetya is the artist for *Blade Bunny*.